CONTENTS

01 | ULSTER CRISIS

The Irish Revolution started in London. Twice in the late nineteenth century, William Ewart Gladstone had sponsored an Irish Home Rule Bill in parliament. The most potent political figure of his time, he had nevertheless failed on both occasions. In 1886, the first bill failed in the House of Commons when his own Liberal Party split on the issue. The second bill, in 1893, passed the Commons but was predictably defeated in the House of Lords.

The House of Lords was one of those peculiar British institutions that made little sense in terms of modern assumptions: it was shamelessly elitist and anti-democratic in what was an ever-more democratising age. It represented privilege, both ancient inherited privilege and that more recently acquired through industrial fortunes. Lordships were created anew as well as inherited. Constitutionally, the House of Lords was the upper house of parliament, a revising chamber which in theory acted as a brake on the more frantic initiatives of the Commons. As was pointed out repeatedly, however, it discharged this function only in respect of bills sponsored by Liberal governments, which it cheerfully emasculated as it thought fit. On Tory legislation, its revising hand palsied.

By the time H.H. Asquith became Liberal Prime Minister in 1908, the House of Lords was nothing more or less than a Conservative barrage, whose sole purpose was to frustrate what it regarded as Liberal legislative excess. The problem for the Lords was that Asquith's government had been elected in one of the biggest landslides in British electoral history. In 1906, the Liberals swept back to power after almost twenty years in the political wilderness. Their leader, Sir Henry Campbell-Bannerman, became Prime Minister and appointed Asquith as Chancellor of the Exchequer. In that position, Asquith displayed the calm assurance that had distinguished his entire career. He introduced old age pensions and other reforms that pre-figured the Welfare State. When Campbell-Bannerman died, Asquith was his unchallenged successor as leader of the party and Prime Minister.

But just why had the Liberals—the party of Gladstone that had completely dominated mid-Victorian politics—come to spend twenty years squabbling with each other on the opposition benches? As always, there were many causes, but none was more central than home rule for Ireland. The split that Gladstone caused by this measure was, more than anything else, responsible for the Liberals' wilderness years. Asquith had first entered parliament in the fateful year of 1886. His whole parliamentary career had therefore overlapped with this period of Liberal decline and division. Unlike Gladstone, Asquith was not a force of nature inspired by high moral ideals. He was a temperate lawyer, wonderfully competent and able. He was shrewd. And like any shrewd Liberal of his era, he remembered all too well the havoc that home rule had brought to his party. In his heart Mr Asquith resolved that here was an issue best avoided.

Not that it was an issue at all in 1908. On the opposition benches in the Commons there sat the members of the Irish Parliamentary Party, the heirs of Parnell. Their numbers were insufficient to influence the government's majority and consequently they could be ignored. The government did introduce an anodyne measure called the Irish Council Bill in 1907, to offer Ireland a very limited form of devolution well short of home rule. It proved far too pallid for the various shades of Irish nationalism—including the IPP—and it was withdrawn.

Their Lordships were growing ever more alarmed by what was coming from the Commons. After a generation of nodding through Conservative measures, they were suddenly galvanised by Liberal legislation. Bills to do with education, plural voting and licensing were all thrown out in the Lords. The Liberals, invested with the legitimacy of a democratic landslide in the Commons, were powerless against their Lordships' naked partisanship.

When Asquith became Prime Minister, his successor as Chancellor was David Lloyd George. Lloyd George was a radical, on the left of the party. He was mercurial and torrentially eloquent. As a small-town Welsh solicitor of an aggressive disposition, he had no love at all for the landed interest that dominated the Lords. In preparing his 1909 budget, he was faced with a large deficit which he was determined to make good. The deficit was caused by increased military spending and by the cost of Asquith's old age pensions. To finance all this, Lloyd George increased income tax and death duties, taxed undeveloped land and mining royalties and imposed heavy duties on the licensed trade, a traditional Tory redoubt. He introduced a super tax on the very rich for the first time. If Lloyd George had set out to select a series of targets designed to infuriate the Tories generally and the House of Lords specifically, he could hardly have done better.

By constitutional convention, the Lords did not reject money bills. Yet here was a money bill that represented a direct assault on their interests, coming at a time when they had grown accustomed to a more assertive use of their veto. After much manoeuvring and agonising, the Lords rejected the 'People's Budget' and tripped off a constitutional crisis.

The two general elections of 1910 were required to resolve it. Twice Asquith went to the country and twice he was returned. Only when he threatened to create enough new peers, all of whom would be safe Liberal placemen, to swamp the existing Tory majority, was the budget finally passed. From this, it was a short legislative step to the Parliament Act of 1911, which finally abolished the Lords' veto, replacing it by a mere power of delay.

The two general elections had, however, caused the configuration of the Commons to change decisively. Asquith had won, but his majority had disappeared and he now found himself, as Gladstone had found himself twenty-five years earlier, depending upon the Irish Parliamentary Party for a secure majority. The IPP was happy to oblige. The condition was obvious. When all was said and done, they were a one-issue party and the issue was home rule. The measure that Asquith least wanted to touch was the one he was made to embrace.

———

Since the 1880s, in every test of political opinion in Ireland, home rule had produced an overwhelming majority. These were reasonably true tests, for a major franchise reform in 1884 had effectively brought all male heads of households in the UK onto the electoral register. There was only one blemish in the image of an Ireland solid for home rule: Ulster.

Ulster, the northern province comprising nine counties, was alone in Ireland in not having an over-whelmingly Catholic population. The province was almost evenly divided between the denominations, although there was a small Catholic majority. The eastern half of Ulster, however, was solidly Protestant. This included the two coastal counties of Antrim and Down and the great industrial city of Belfast. As one pushed west from this heartland, however, Protestant numbers weakened although still able to command local electoral majorities in many areas. The two most southerly Ulster counties, Cavan and Monaghan, and the most westerly (ironically, also the most northerly), Donegal, contained very substantial Catholic majorities.

Catholic meant nationalist and pro-home rule. Protestant meant unionist and anti-home rule. It really was as simple as that. The few exceptions here and there were of no account and statistically insignificant. Irish nationalism was an overtly Catholic project and Irish unionism a Protestant one. There was some small support for unionism among a tiny minority of southern upper-middle class Catholics, but in Ulster the overlap between confessional allegiance and political allegiance was nearly total.

The electoral map of Ulster in December 1910 was a perfect reflection of this confessional demography. With just a single exception, every constituency in the three most heavily Protestant counties—Antrim, Down and Derry—returned the Unionist candidate. The exception was South Down, which had a secure local Catholic majority. And so it went throughout Ulster, with the Protestant constituencies of North and Mid Armagh, South Tyrone and North Fermanagh declaring for the

Unionists while the rest of the province—effectively most of west Ulster—remained overwhelmingly Nationalist. The farther south and west one went in Ulster, the more certain the Nationalist majority. The election of December 1910 simply underlined the immutable electoral geography of the province, visible in all elections since 1885.

Ulster was divided, with the Protestant heartland in the east centred on Belfast. But there was more to power than counting heads. The Protestant community in Ulster was vastly richer, more influential and more confident than the Catholics. The Industrial Revolution had touched Ulster alone in Ireland, and within Ulster it had been a Protestant phenomenon. Theirs was the community that had been enriched by it. Even among the Protestant working class, there were more skilled tradesmen than among the Catholics, who swelled the ranks of the unskilled or the unemployed in disproportionate numbers. The Protestant poor knew themselves to be part of a superior caste. As for the middle class, it was substantially Protestant.

Sir James Craig was the very epitome of the new Ulster plutocrat. He was the hatchet-faced heir to a distillery, very rich and from 1906 a Unionist MP at Westminster. He was meticulous. He was no orator and had little charisma, but he was at the heart of every Unionist intrigue in this period. One month before the election of December 1910, he was one of those on the Ulster Unionist Council who authorised the setting up of a secret committee to buy arms from abroad with a view to forming an Ulster army to resist home rule.

This was the Rubicon moment.

——

One of the great ironies of the Irish Revolution is that it was started by those who least wanted it. The Ulster unionists wanted nothing more than the status quo, the maintenance of the union of Great Britain and Ireland that had subsisted since 1801. Their faith in parliament had been well placed for a generation, but now all that was changing. Since home rule first became an issue in the mid-1880s, Ulster could always rely on the House of Lords to torpedo any proposed legislation. By November 1910, however, the danger of a Liberal government beholden to the Irish Parliamentary Party for its majority was sufficiently real to push the Ulster Unionist Council over the brink. The Parliament Act was already over the horizon, set to remove the Lords' veto and therefore the surest bulwark against home rule. In forming the secret committee to buy arms and plan armed resistance to the will of parliament, the UUC was on the path of treason. And that is what the Ulster Crisis was all about: treason in defence of the constitution.

The work of securing arms for the putative Ulster army was devolved to one of those exotics who seem to flash across the Edwardian stage as if it were a music hall. Major Frederick Hugh Crawford had been at the wilder margins of Ulster unionism since the early 1890s.

A UVF rally in June 1914: Sir Edward Carson acknowledges the cheers of the crowd. *Photograph reproduced with the kind permission of the Trustees of the National Museums Northern Ireland*

As a member of the Ulster Loyalist Union—formed to focus opposition to the first two Home Rule Bills—he had imported arms from England and organised the drilling of volunteers. On the strength of all this, he founded an armed society called Young Ulster which toyed briefly with the idea of kidnapping Gladstone, at that time eighty-four and in his fourth and final term as Prime Minister. He later saw more orthodox service as an officer in the Boer War. This was the person to whom the Ulster Unionist Council devolved the business of arming Protestant Ulster.

With the return of Asquith and the passing of the Parliament Act, the UUC plunged ever deeper in. As early as March 1911, it was committing funds to Crawford's enterprise. The first arms had been secured by the summer of that year. As early as April, a body of armed Orangemen in military formation had presented themselves at a rally in Craigavon, Sir James Craig's splendid country house outside Belfast. The paramilitary mobilisation would continue to gather pace throughout 1911 and 1912.

In the meantime, the political game moved on. Craig was the Ulster Carnot, the 'organiser of victory', but he was no leader and he knew it. Instead, he turned to Edward Carson to assume the leadership of the anti-home rule cause. Carson was an inspired if unlikely choice. He was not from Ulster, but from Dublin. He was born into a prosperous professional family—his father was a successful architect—and he himself became a barrister. He practised at first in Ireland, where he made a reputation for himself as a tough crown prosecutor during the land agitations of the 1880s. This brought him to the notice of the Chief Secretary, Arthur Balfour, nephew of the Prime Minister and later to be leader of the Tory party and Prime Minister himself. He was called to the English Bar in 1893, one year after his election to the House of Commons as MP for his *alma mater*, Trinity College. He was appointed solicitor-general for Ireland and later solicitor-general for England (1900–05). But his most celebrated and notorious achievement had been not in politics but at the Bar. In 1895, he was counsel for the defence in the libel action taken by Oscar Wilde against the Marquess of Queensberry, the father of Wilde's lover Lord Alfred Douglas. His destruction of Wilde in cross-examination confirmed his reputation as one of the most feared and respected lawyers in Britain.

The Unionists had therefore just found a leader from the heart of the Conservative establishment. Notwithstanding this background, Carson was under no illusions about guns. On the contrary, lawyer or no lawyer, he saw them as essential to the course that the Ulster resistance was now embarked upon. As a southern unionist, Carson saw Ulster as the rock upon which home rule would break, for he reckoned that if Ulster could stay out, the whole enterprise would collapse. Carson's concern was for Ireland in the union, not just Ulster. Like most of his contemporaries, he simply could not imagine the island partitioned, so complete was the mental image of insular unity.

Carson made his first major speech as Unionist leader in September 1911, once again at a rally in Craigavon. There was no ambiguity: 'We must be prepared, on the morning home rule passes, ourselves to become responsible for the government of the Protestant province of Ulster.' If this was not a threat of de facto secession, what was it? Yet the lawyer in Carson was nothing if not subtle and ambiguous. Behind the scenes, he used his well-oiled political connections to try to reach successive accommodations with the government, while stirring up his Ulster audiences with inflammatory public speeches of great force and power. Carson was playing an Irish political game as old as Daniel O'Connell—he would hardly have welcomed the comparison—by using his control of the outraged mob as a lever to extract concessions from a frightened government.

Throughout 1911 and 1912, the process of political mobilisation, occasional importation of arms and drilling continued apace in Ulster. Drilling was illegal unless granted a permit by a magistrate, but since most of the magistrates were unionist in sympathy, that little formality was seldom a problem. The threat against which it was all focused was made flesh in the House of Commons on 11 April 1912 when Asquith introduced the Third Home Rule Bill, a moment that prompted John Redmond, the leader of the Irish Parliamentary Party, to thank God that he had lived to see the day. It was, incidentally, just three days before the sinking of the *Titanic*.

With the safety net of the House of Lords now gone, Ulster was thrown entirely upon its own resources. Well, almost. The Conservatives were demoralised after the passage of the People's Budget and the Parliament Act, and in November 1911 Balfour had been forced aside in favour of a very different type of leader, Andrew Bonar Law. He had been born in Canada and brought up in Glasgow and significantly was of mixed Ulster and Scots background. His father had been born in Coleraine and had been the Presbyterian minister there before leaving for Canada. Where Balfour had been a southern grandee, Bonar Law was closer in knowledge, sympathy and formation to the tough Presbyterian ethic of the Ulster Protestants with whom he shared a visceral sympathy. Bonar Law's arrival as Tory leader deepened the overt bond of sympathy and co-operation between the Ulster Unionists and the Conservative Party. He shared platforms with Carson and injected an element of righteous fury to the British anti-home rule opposition that sat very easily with the Ulstermen.

Bonar Law was the incarnation of growing British Tory opposition to home rule, most memorably captured in Kipling's poem 'Ulster 1912'. At Easter that year, as the Home Rule Bill was being introduced in the Commons, he spoke to a loyalist crowd of over 100,000 in Belfast. Prayers were read by the Anglican primate and the Presbyterian moderator. Hymns were sung, resolutions against home rule were passed, and the largest Union flag ever made was flown aloft. Bonar Law spoke from the heart: 'Once again you hold the pass, the pass for Empire. You are a besieged city. The timid have left you. Your Lundys have betrayed you, but you have closed your gates. The government have erected by their Parliament Act a boom against you to shut you off from the help of the British people. You will burst that boom.'

This overt series of references to the siege of Derry in 1690, a moment of resistance that was central to the Ulster Protestant historical imagination, was no accident. (Lundy was the governor of Derry who had thought resistance futile.) In the end, the isolated Protestant garrison, besieged for 105 days by Jacobites, had been rescued by a ship that burst the Jacobite boom across the Foyle river and brought supplies and relief to the town. For Bonar Law's audience, this was stirring, emotional stuff establishing a direct connection with heroic ancestors. Nor did Law reserve his bravura rhetoric for easily swayed Ulster audiences. Later that summer, in England, he declared unambiguously that 'I can imagine no lengths of resistance to which Ulster can go in which I would not be prepared to support her.' This man was the Leader of His Majesty's Loyal Opposition.

On 28 September 1912, Carson and Craig pulled off a stunning *coup de theatre*. They had declared this to be Ulster Day and for it they prepared Ulster's Solemn League and Covenant, a declaration couched in suitably Biblical rhetoric which read in full as follows:

> *Being convinced in our consciences that home rule would be disastrous to the material well-being of Ulster as well as to the whole of Ireland, subversive of our civil and religious freedom, destructive of our citizenship*

*and perilous to the unity of the Empire, we, whose
names are underwritten, men of Ulster, loyal subjects
of His Gracious Majesty King George V, humbly relying
on the God whom our fathers in days of stress and trial
confidently trusted, do hereby pledge ourselves in
Solemn Covenant throughout this our time of threatened calamity to stand by one another in defending for
ourselves and our children our cherished position of
equal citizenship in the United Kingdom and in using
all means which may be found necessary to defeat the
present conspiracy to set up a Home Rule Parliament
in Ireland. And in the event of such a Parliament being
forced upon us we further solemnly and mutually
pledge ourselves to refuse to recognise its authority. In
sure confidence that God will defend the right we hereto
subscribe our names. And further, we individually
declare that we have not already signed this Covenant.*

The above was signed by me at _____

Ulster Day, Saturday 28th, September, 1912.

God Save the King

This document was signed first by Carson at a table set
up in the vestibule of the City Hall, Belfast, and covered
in the Union flag. In all, 237,368 men signed the
Covenant that day, some in their own blood. A total of
234,046 women signed a similar document, highlighting
a relatively neglected aspect of the Ulster Crisis, the very
full part played by women. The clarity of the language
in the Covenant speaks for itself, as does the plain
determination of those who drafted it and signed it. The

language is Biblical in tone, but the document contains a further religious context that would have resonated easily in Protestant Ulster. The original Solemn League and Covenant of 1643 was an agreement made between Scots Presbyterians and English Dissenters to join forces in the Civil War against King Charles I. Thus it could be represented as a union of the virtuous against the impious forces of overweening authority. This is roughly how the Ulster Protestants saw themselves in 1912.

On New Year's Day 1913, an amendment to the Third Home Rule Bill, to exclude Ulster from its provisions, was defeated. It was not the first such proposal: in the previous June, an amendment in the name of a Liberal MP, T.G. Agar-Robertes, had proposed the exclusion of the four most Protestant counties of Ulster: Antrim, Down, Derry and Armagh. It too was defeated, but these were significant amendments. Faced with the implacable advance of the nationalist demand and the adamantine resistance of the unionists, the possibility of partition as a solution was being raised for the first time. By 16 January, home rule was through the Commons. The Lords wasted no time over it: by the 30th, they had thrown it out. But thanks to the Parliament Act, their power was now only one of delay. In two years, there would be home rule for Ireland.

The very next day, the Ulster Volunteer Force was formed. This formalised what had been happening on the ground among the various drilling militias over the previous two years and brought them under a central command. In turn, the leadership of the UVF was under the control of the leadership of the Ulster Unionist Party. This was no rag-tag force. It numbered almost 90,000 men and its officers were retired British Army personnel, including such luminaries as the commander, General Sir George Richardson, and Captain Wilfrid Spender. For its first year of life, the UVF had very few arms and had to rely on wooden dummies instead. But always in the background, beavering away, was Fred Crawford. In little more than a year, his efforts were to transform the situation, as we shall see.

By September 1913, 500 delegates to the Ulster Unionist Council approved the establishment of a Provisional Government of Ulster to be chaired by Sir Edward Carson. It met for the first time on 10 July 1914, just weeks before the world collapsed into war and shelved the Ulster impasse for four years. But it was a further raising of the stakes for all concerned. In December 1913, the government pronounced a ban on the importation of arms into Ireland.

The government supposed, naively as it turned out, that this eliminated any threat of arms from abroad being shipped into Ireland in support of militias, whether unionist or nationalist. Ulster was their main concern, and they now grew worried that the UVF might attempt to raid army arms depots in the province in order to arm themselves. Accordingly, the War Office in London gave instructions to Major-General Sir Arthur Paget, the commander-in-chief of the British Army in Ireland, to prepare plans for the movement of troops to protect the depots. Paget was stationed at the Curragh, about thirty-five miles south of Dublin. He foolishly let it be known that officers domiciled in Ulster could simply look the other way and would not be forced to move against their own province and people. All other officers would be expected to obey orders in the normal manner. At this, Brigadier-General Sir Hubert Gough, officer commanding the 3rd Cavalry Brigade, called a meeting which resulted in sixty officers offering to resign their commissions rather than have any part in coercing loyal Ulster. The fact that any such action was for the protection of army property and matériel and the maintenance of the law seems not to have occurred to them or, if it did, it did not weigh very heavily with them.

Gough led a delegation to see General Sir Henry Wilson, the Director of Military Operations and a deep-dyed Tory ultra, in London. The War Office refused the offers of resignation, stating that the government intended to take no offensive action against Ulster. This statement was made without government authority and the subsequent furore brought the resignations of the Chief of the Imperial General Staff, Field-Marshal Sir John French, the Adjutant-General, Sir Spencer Ewart, and the Secretary of State for War, Colonel John Seely.

These were not little players and their defenestration shows just what a serious matter the Curragh Mutiny was. Some historians have preferred to call it the Curragh Incident, on the quibbling pretext that no direct orders were disobeyed. That is sophistry. The Irish poison had run so far in the British bloodstream

A reconstruction of the Larne Gun Running first published in the *Illustrated London News*. In this painting, the name of the ship (not visible in this reproduction), the *Mountjoy*, was a deliberate error. The actual ship was the *Clyde Valley*, but the *Mountjoy* had been the ship that raised the siege of Derry in 1689. It was a potent reminder for Ulster Protestants of supposed historical continuity. *The Illustrated London News Picture Library*

that for the first time since 1688 the civil power could not depend on the army to do its bidding.

Barely a month after the Curragh Mutiny, the arms depots became largely irrelevant. On the night of 24–25 April 1914, the UVF landed 25,000 rifles and 3 million rounds of ammunition at Larne, Co. Antrim, in an operation conducted with military precision and no little collusion from the authorities. It was not nearly enough to arm all of the UVF and it contained different types of guns and ammunition rather than standard ordnance. The UVF, post-Larne, was still not a potent fighting force, although it could certainly have conducted a local guerrilla war if things had come to that. But most of all, the Larne gun-running, the product of nearly four years labour on Fred Crawford's part, was a statement of political capacity and intent. The guns were transhipped onto the *Clyde Valley*, an old rust bucket that Crawford had bought in Glasgow, off the Tuskar Rock at the south-east corner of the island. It nearly ended in farce, as the *Clyde Valley* was almost capsized by the wake from a passing Royal Navy warship racing down St George's Channel. But Crawford's luck held. He got the guns ashore at Larne and gave the Ulster cause a huge psychological boost. It gave Asquith yet another headache.

The cumulative effect of these events in the first half of 1914 pushed the government ever more despairingly towards some attempt to reconcile the irreconcilable opposites. With home rule enacted and awaiting enablement, with the army uncertain after the Curragh, with the stony determination of Protestant Ulster in no doubt after Larne (not that there had been much doubt before), with Bonar Law's Tories shoulder-to-shoulder with Carson, it seemed that something had to give. Lloyd George suggested that Ulster counties with Protestant majorities could opt out of home rule for the first six years, an offer spurned by Carson as 'a sentence of death with a stay of execution for six years'.

Finally, at the last minute of the eleventh hour, the Buckingham Palace Conference of July 1914 was an attempt by King George V to bring all the principals together in a final search for an accommodation. The rather touching British belief in the endless potential of compromise solutions hit a brick wall in three days. Asquith and Lloyd George; Law and the Tories; Redmond and John Dillon from the IPP; Craig and Carson: they were all there under the chairmanship of the Speaker of the Commons. The intractable question of Ulster simply could not be neutralised by a formula. The impasse that had prompted the conference was too great.

It is impossible for us to re-create the mid-summer of 1914 as contemporaries saw it. We know that they stood on the volcano's edge. The war that broke out less than a fortnight after the end of the Buckingham Palace Conference transformed everything. Home Rule became law in September but was suspended until the end of the war, by which time it was irrelevant. The UVF became the 36th Ulster Division of the British Army and were slaughtered on the first day of the Battle of the

Somme. Nationalist Ireland's demands became more radical and urgent under the pressure of a new generation. It is to the nationalist side that we turn next.

Before we do, it is worth reflecting on the Ulster Crisis. In one sense, in the palpable existence of Northern Ireland, it is with us still. In terms of its contribution to the Irish Revolution, however, it seems to me to have two critical elements. First, under pressure from Protestant resistance to home rule, the very question of partition—literally unthinkable before 1910—slowly seeped into the world of possibility. From Agar-Robertes' proposal in May 1912 to Lloyd George's 'sentence of death with a stay for six years' was less than two years. In that time, the pressure of events got the previously unthinkable on to the political agenda.

Second, the Ulster Crisis fatally compromised the legitimacy of British government in Ireland in the eyes of nationalists. That legitimacy had always been partial and uncertain, but it is worth recalling that had home rule been enacted, the Union flag would still have flown over the GPO in O'Connell Street. By the end of the war, that possibility seemed as ludicrous as partition had seemed a decade earlier. In nationalist eyes, the British establishment had indulged the unionists. The Tories were openly colluding with their illegalities. The army could not be relied upon. The law of the land was being defied and government ministers could only urge wheedling compromises on the perpetrators, compromises which they summarily rejected. The whole progress of the Ulster Crisis might have been designed to erode nationalist belief in British good faith. It was fatal to those elements in Irish nationalism that had reposed hope in that good faith.

02 | NATIONALISM BEFORE 1916

Mr John Redmond was the man of the hour. It was January 1911 and the last few results from the UK general election of December 1910 had been declared. Asquith's Liberals had secured 272 seats. The Tories and their Liberal Unionist allies had 271. Redmond, with 74 members and another ten Irish Nationalists who did not formally take the party whip but could be relied upon on the big issue, held the balance of power. The big issue was home rule.

It was 1886 all over again. In that year, Parnell—the political genius who had effectively founded the Irish Parliamentary Party—had held the balance of power. As his price for supporting Gladstone, he had extracted from the Prime Minister a promise to do something considered at the time by all conventional opinion to be a political impossibility and a nonsense: the granting of

John Redmond at the height of his influence. *Hulton Archive/Getty Images*

home rule to Ireland. The result was the First Home Rule Bill. It failed; it split the Liberals. But none of that seemed to matter. Home rule was now part of the British political vernacular. Sooner or later, it was bound to happen.

Four years later, the IPP tore itself apart over Parnell's private life. The Parnell split poisoned Irish political life for years. It took ten years for the pro- and anti-Parnell factions to agree, rather nervously, to re-unite the party. As a gesture of goodwill, the majority conceded the leadership of the reunited party to the most prominent member in the minority faction, John Redmond.

Redmond was the son and grand-nephew of MPs. Born in Ballytrent House, Co. Wexford, in 1856 he was a member of the small Catholic elite disproportionately concentrated in the south-east of Ireland. He was educated at Clongowes, the most exclusive Jesuit school in Ireland, and at Trinity. He became a barrister, but politics soon beckoned. He entered the House of Commons as MP for New Ross, Co. Wexford, in 1880. He was to spend the rest of his life as an MP for three different south-eastern constituencies.

Although a nationalist and a supporter of Parnell, he had certain personal associations that set him apart from the general run of nationalists. His mother was Protestant. Mixed marriages, especially for members of the Catholic elite, were not as unusual as they later became but they were by no means common. Redmond married twice: his first wife was Australian, his second English. He was, therefore, not suffused in the claustrophobic embrace of all things Irish in a manner similar to many of his party colleagues. For most of his career, his home was in London, although he had a country house in Co. Wicklow. When he came to Dublin, he stayed in a hotel.

Among Redmond's colleagues, none was more important than John Dillon. Like Redmond, Dillon was born to the nationalist purple. He was the son of John Blake Dillon, one of the founders of *The Nation* newspaper in the 1840s. It was an overnight sensation and for years thereafter the premier nationalist organ. Dillon *père* was a barrister and a radical: a supporter of the Young Ireland movement and a leader of the ill-fated Rising of 1848. Having escaped to New York, he returned to Ireland in 1855 under the terms of an amnesty. His son, born in 1851, came therefore from a background more inclined to radicalism than the very gentlemanly Redmond. John Dillon qualified as a doctor, although he did not practise. His early radicalism marked him out as one of the most militant agrarian agitators of the 1880s: he had a lifelong hatred of landlords and the system of land ownership that sustained them. He spent four separate terms in prison in the 1880s and was a strong supporter of the Plan of Campaign, a land agitation in the second half of that decade of which Parnell disapproved (in his eyes, it was distracting from the politics of home rule). All his life, he retained that edge of urgent radicalism, perhaps reflecting his West of Ireland background. He had been born in Co. Mayo and sat as MP for that impoverished county from 1885 until the tidal wave of 1918 carried the IPP into history.

It was this pair, the bland Redmond from the lush

south-east and Dillon the radical from Mayo, who made a formidable double act at the head of Irish parliamentary nationalism from 1900—the year the party was re-united after the Parnell split—until 1914. Dillon had stood aside to allow Redmond assume the leadership of the party. Although not personally close, they understood that by forming an unshakeable alliance they were beyond the reach of all internal opposition. And so it was.

The 1900s was not a promising decade for them. They had no parliamentary leverage. First the Tories under Balfour were in power until 1905, then the Liberal land-slide marginalised them. Until 1910, that is. The two elections of that year produced almost identical results, leaving the IPP holding the balance of power. Mr Redmond was the man of the hour.

———

He was the man of the hour if you were standing on Westminster bridge, less so if you were on O'Connell bridge. It is not that he did not have huge—indeed over-whelming—support in Ireland. He did. But there were forces stirring that were outside Redmond's imaginative orbit, and although they seemed of little consequence in January 1911, they would do for him in the end.

A few months earlier, James Connolly had published two books: *Labour in Irish History* and *Labour, Nationality and Religion.* The first, in particular, was a full-blooded challenge to the traditional nationalist

John Dillon, for long Redmond's loyal deputy, finally inherited the leadership of the Irish Party when it was a busted flush. *RTÉ Stills Library*

historical narrative. It interpreted the Irish past in Marxist terms, as a series of internal class struggles in which the economic interests of the weakest were serially betrayed by the strong. The strong included the middle-class leadership of Irish nationalism, not least the IPP: Connolly had no time for Redmond. Instead, Connolly tried to rescue an imagined communitarian Irish tradition from the distant Celtic past in which land and goods were held in common. This fanciful interpretation of Celtic socio-economics was employed in the service of Connolly's contemporary politics. Connolly was a revolutionary, and one of the most remarkable men of his time.

He had been born in an Edinburgh slum in 1868 and had all the passionate certainty of the autodidact that he was. He first came to Dublin to organise the city's social-ist society in 1896 and became a delegate to the Dublin Trades Council. He founded a small socialist republican party and in 1902 was invited to the United States to give a series of lectures. Gilded-age America seemed to him a far more promising field for socialist agitation than moribund Ireland and he spent the next eight years there. He returned in July 1910 to take up a position in the recently founded Irish Transport & General Workers' Union.

The IT&GWU was the creation of James Larkin, the most charismatic labour leader in Britain and Ireland. Liverpool-Irish, physically imposing, a spell-binding platform speaker and a convinced syndicalist, in 1907 he had organised a dock strike in Belfast on behalf of the National Union of Dock Labourers, whose headquarters were in London. It was a bitter, protracted affair, eventually settled by the union leadership over Larkin's head on conditions that he regarded as a betrayal. It was this experience that prompted him to establish the IT&GWU, an independent Irish union. It had a further characteristic that set it apart from most existing British and Irish unions: it aimed to mobilise the unskilled. Most traditional trade unions were aimed at skilled and semi-skilled workers. It was no accident that the body on which James Connolly had been a delegate back in 1896 had been called the Dublin Trades Council. Trades unions were for skilled tradesmen first and foremost: the unskilled could shift for themselves.

Larkin's IT&GWU changed all that. Moreover, it introduced syndicalism into Ireland. The word derived from 'syndicat', the French for trade union. Syndicalism sought the enfeeblement and destruction of capitalism through large federated unions—rather than the separate series of craft unions that were then the norm—leading to the ultimate dispossession of capitalist ownership and the vesting of the means of production and exchange in the hands of the workers. It was therefore an overtly aggressive interpretation of Marxist theory. Its preferred weapon was the sympathetic strike, whereby a big federated union with workers in all branches of industry and commerce could paralyse a whole economy in support of strikers in a single sector. It was no accident that when Larkin formed the IT&GWU, the slogan he chose for it was OBU: one big union.

Connolly had also been exposed to syndicalism while

in America, but it was a doctrine that was hitherto unknown in the UK where a tradition of cautious compromise—and a suspicion of fancy French theory—ran deep. Between them, Larkin and Connolly had a transforming effect on Ireland—especially on Dublin. In 1912, they founded the Irish Labour Party, still the oldest political party in the Republic (although not on the island: the Ulster Unionist Party pre-dates it by at least seven years). In 1913, they presided over the greatest labour dispute in Irish history, the Lockout of 1913.

Dublin was a city of teeming slums. About 100,000 people, perhaps a third of the entire city population, lived in what were reckoned by contemporaries to be the most sordid and insanitary conditions in northern Europe, worse even than the notorious Gorbals district of Glasgow. Georgian town houses, built for the Anglo-Irish grandees of the eighteenth century who had progressively decamped to London after the Act of Union, had fallen into the hands of unscrupulous *rentiers*, many of them Catholics, nationalists and supporters of the IPP. Into these properties, they stuffed the abundant poor. The following quotation, from a source hostile to the trade union movement, tells its own tale:

> *The Dublin slum is a thing apart in the inferno of social degradation…. In buildings, old, rotten and permeated with both physical and moral corruption—they crowd in incredible numbers. At the Government Inquiry into Dublin housing conditions held in November and December 1913, some astounding facts*

were brought to public prominence relative to the extent to which human beings are herded together in the Irish capital. Altogether, there appears to be in the city 5,322 tenement houses, accommodating, if such a word can be used, 25,822 families, or a total population of 87,205. No fewer than 20,108 families occupy one room each, 4,402 of the remainder have only two rooms each. But this is only part of the terrible record.

In the official report of the inquiry, the houses are divided into three classes: (a) houses which appear structurally sound; (b) houses which are so decayed, or so badly constructed, as to be on or fast approaching the border-line of being unfit for human habitation; (c) houses unfit for human habitation…. In the first category are included 1,516 tenements occupied by 8,295 families and by 27,052 persons. The second, dubious class comprises 2,288 tenements occupied by 10,696 families and 37,552 persons. In the last section of all are included 1,518 tenements occupied by 6,831 families and 22,701 persons…. We might say, without any overstatement, that the majority of the occupiers of these tenement houses … live under conditions which are injurious to physique and morality.

Indeed he might, and this from a history of the Lockout commissioned by the employers! The Lockout itself was a battle of wills between Larkin and the most powerful employer in Dublin, William Martin Murphy. He was the owner of the Dublin United Tramway Company, which ran the city's public transport system. He was also the proprietor of the *Irish Catholic* and *Irish Independent* newspapers, a director of two railway companies and president of the Dublin Chamber of Commerce. He had been a Nationalist MP from 1885 to 1892 and was a supporter of the brilliant maverick MP, Timothy Healy, to whom he was related—a Nationalist who, for reasons of personality and policy, was excluded from the inner circle of the Redmond-Dillon axis.

Murphy hated Larkin. But he knew enough to mimic Larkin's talent for combination and so he formed an Employers' Federation with himself at the head of it. He then demanded that all his employees give a written assurance that they would not join Larkin's union. A hundred who had already done so and who refused to back down were dismissed. Larkin called out the tramway workers, paralysing the transport system during Horse Show week, one of the social highlights of the year. With that, the employers locked the men out and the IT&GWU responded with a series of sympathetic strikes. By the end of September 1913, more than 20,000 men were out: either on strike or locked out.

It was a vicious business. At the end of August, a rally of strikers in O'Connell Street was baton charged by the Dublin Metropolitan Police, resulting in two deaths and scores of injuries. Workers ('scabs') brought in by the employers to fill some jobs were intimidated. An ingenious scheme by Larkin to send slum children to England for a fortnight's holiday—where they would stay with union families and be fed, something they could not rely on at home in the midst of the privations being borne

One of the many 'Bloody Sundays' in modern Irish history. On 31 August 1913, striking and locked out workers were batoned in central Dublin by the Dublin Metropolitan Police. *RTÉ Stills Library*

by the strikers—was frustrated in the most astonishing way. Parties of Catholic vigilantes, including many priests, succeeded in preventing the children from boarding boats and trains, lest their faith be contaminated in English Protestant homes! All this despite the fact that the consent of the parents had been sought and obtained in every case. To be fair, there were some in the trade union movement who thought the scheme a stunt in bad taste and an example of Larkin's poor judgment in making an enemy of the Catholic Church in the middle of a life-or-death labour dispute. At any rate, the children were prevented from going by this illegal orgy of intimidation, leaving Larkin sourly to remark that it was a poor religion that couldn't stand two weeks holiday in England. Not that Larkin was any paragon: his paper, the *Irish Worker*, had not scrupled to carry anti-Semitic content in the past, including one very nasty cartoon captioned 'Gentlemen of the Jewry' and featuring a bloated capitalist named Ikey O'Moses.

In the end, the men were starved back. It was the Belfast dock strike of 1907 in reprise. The British trade unionists, never comfortable with the volcanic Larkin, gradually reduced their aid to the IT&GWU and by early 1914 the men were returning to work on the best terms they could get. Larkin left for America, not to return for nine years. Connolly took over the union. But in the course of the dispute, he had formed a small militia for the protection of workers following the DMP's baton charge. The Irish Citizen Army was a small affair, but we shall see more of it in due course.

James Larkin. This photograph was taken shortly before the 1913 Lockout.
Bettmann/Corbis

It is worth noting that the workers drew little or no support from mainstream nationalists or from nationalist ginger groups outside the ambit of the IPP. Even these groups tended to be overwhelmingly bourgeois, suspicious of militant labour, suspicious of its international (for which read British) links and concerned to develop indigenous Irish commerce. These were not concerns likely to induce a deep sympathy for working-class agitation, especially when conducted in the grand operatic manner favoured by Larkin, around whom lightnings flashed. He had his faults, Larkin, but he set himself against great evils to which others were indifferent. Perhaps the last word on him should be left to Sean O'Casey, who adored him, recalling the first time he heard him speak:

> *From a window in the building [Liberty Hall], leaning well forth, he talked to the workers, spoke only as Jim Larkin could speak, not for an assignation with peace, dark obedience, or placid resignation; but trumpet-tongued of resistance to wrong, discontent with leering poverty, and defiance of any power strutting out to stand in the way of their march onward.*

Not the least of the marginal nationalist groups outside the ambit of the IPP was Sinn Féin. But like many other groups that were regarded, quite rightly, as marginal at the time, it later became central—indeed, the name is with us still, although the modern version is a world removed from the original. The movement of various bodies and parties from the margins of life to the centre in a short period is the essence of the Irish Revolution.

Sinn Féin began as a concept, not a party. In Irish, it simply means 'ourselves', not 'ourselves alone' as it is so often mistranslated. It was the product of the fertile mind of a gifted, acerbic journalist called Arthur Griffith. He came of age around the time of the Parnell split and shared a generational sense of disgust with the shabby manoeuvrings of the IPP after that disaster. By the time the party had re-united in 1900, Griffith was almost thirty. He had looked back beyond the squalor of the IPP to the idealism of the Young Ireland movement of the 1840s—the one of which John Dillon's father had been a luminary. Above all, he was entranced by the non-sectarianism of the poet Thomas Davis. Likewise, he drew on a very different Young Irelander, the bitterly Anglophobic John Mitchel whose *Jail Journal* was and is a classic of nationalist political literature. Mitchel was a great hater. Griffith's politics were a search for an accommodation between Davis and Mitchel.

He was involved in everything as a young man: literary clubs, debating societies, drama groups, the committee celebrating the centenary of the 1798 Rising (of which incidentally he disapproved), the anti-Boer War campaign, opposition to the visit of Queen Victoria in 1900, and so on. He was autodidactic like many lower middle-class men of his generation. He differed from his contemporary, James Connolly, in the influences he absorbed, although each was unusual in his concern with economics: this in a culture that ran easily, perhaps too easily, to politics. Where Connolly was a Marxist, Griffith was a follower of the German-American economic theorist Friedrich List. Originally a disciple of Adam Smith, List moderated his views of classical free trade economics to stress the supreme importance of the nation as the basic unit of economic development. This inevitably led to an emphasis on protection, national tariffs and the development of indigenous industry. List's theories were influential among countries experiencing the second wave of the industrial revolution—not least his native Germany—because they facilitated development. It was all very well for Britain to be a noisy sponsor of pure free trade, since she was first in the field. For countries lagging behind and anxious to catch up, List had an enormous appeal. That was what Griffith found in his work.

He founded a newspaper, the *United Irishman*, in 1899. It was re-launched seven years later as *Sinn Féin*. In that time, he set forth a series of constitutional, economic and political prescriptions that were regarded as mildly potty by mainstream nationalists but were to prove of enduring influence. He was the first to propose that Irish MPs abstain from Westminster and run for office on a frankly abstentionist ticket. He proposed a dual monarchy solution based on the Austro-Hungarian model (it also harked back to Grattan's Parliament in the eighteenth century, the one abolished by the Act of

Union, which Griffith admired in a rather starry-eyed way). He crystallised this proposal in *The Resurrection of Hungary: A Parallel for Ireland*, first published as a series of twenty-seven articles in the *United Irishman* in 1904 and issued in book form later that year.

In 1905, Griffith founded Sinn Féin. It went through a series of mutations over the next three years, absorbing other small nationalist groups before emerging as a recognisable party in 1908. By one of those ironies that are the spice of history, the name was suggested by Mary Lambert Butler, a cousin of Sir Edward Carson. The little party created a minor stir by gathering 1,157 votes in a by-election in North Leitrim in 1908, although it never seriously challenged the IPP candidate. There were local factors at play in the vote: the Sinn Féin candidate was himself a former IPP MP with a personal following; and local unionists (irony of ironies) probably voted for Sinn Féin, on the principle of anyone except the IPP.

Sinn Féin's modest showing in North Leitrim took it nowhere in particular. It did not contest another election of any kind until after the 1916 Rising, when it had undergone a further huge mutation that made it unrecognisable from the feeble creature at the margins of nationalist politics. The reason for its occlusion was simple enough. After January 1910, the IPP was back in business, holding the balance of power at Westminster. John Redmond was the man of the hour.

————

The period between the fall of Parnell and the 1916 Rising was the golden age of the Irish cultural revival. In 1893, the Gaelic League was founded by Douglas Hyde and Eoin Mac Neill in order to revive and protect the Irish language as a spoken vernacular. It arose out of a paper delivered by Hyde in the previous year un-ambiguously entitled 'The Necessity for de-Anglicising Ireland'. Hyde's views were trenchant expressions of cultural separatism: 'It is a most disgraceful shame the way in which Irishmen are brought up. They are ashamed of their language, institutions, and of every-thing Irish.' And again: 'Reverence for our past history, regard for the memory of our ancestors, our national honour, and the fear of becoming materialized and losing our best and highest characteristics call upon us imperatively to assist the Irish-speaking population.'

The Gaelic League was a huge success among the idealistic young. The character of Miss Ivors in Joyce's great short story 'The Dead', she who did not wear a low-cut bodice, whose brooch bore an Irish device and motto and who chastised the protagonist for being a West Briton, was a good example of the type. The League was a numerous organisation, especially after 1908, but never a mass one. Its influence resided in the kind of person it attracted: the post-Parnell generation of educated and ambitious nationalists, although it was in its early days genuinely non-sectarian and, as far as it was possible to be in Ireland, non-political. Hyde was himself the son of a Church of Ireland rector. Still, its cultural emphasis more readily inclined to separatism than to unionism and its historic importance resides in its being a forcing house for a new nationalist elite.

The involvement of Protestants and unionists in the cultural revival has often been explained by the view that the more perceptive among them recognised that with the disestablishment of the Church of Ireland (1869), the imminence of home rule and the break-up of the great landed estates in the first decade of the twentieth century, the game was up for the old order. It was necessary both to shape the new Ireland and to bend to it. Whatever the value of this insight, the Protestant contribution to the years between 1891 and 1916 was immense. Yeats, Lady Gregory, Synge, O'Casey, Hyde, Standish O'Grady and a score of others left a permanent mark on the Ireland that was in gestation. And the greatest of these was Yeats.

Yeats was the finest English-language poet of his time, a man of action in the theatre, in later life a Senator, a man consumed with a passion for the mysterious and the numinous, a hater of bourgeois materialism, and a seemingly paradoxical supporter of both the aristocratic principle and radical republicanism. (This last is not as paradoxical as it seems: he was a cultural and political Samurai.) His Ireland of Big Houses and virtuous peasants was exactly what was disappearing before his eyes in his own lifetime. Everything he celebrated as positive in his native country was being elbowed aside by the incremental materialism of the Irish lower middle class on the march. Yeats did not do sociology.

That said, Yeats' contribution was beyond measure. He gave the Irish nation—or at least his mental image of it—the pride of an unsurpassed poetry, this in a country where poets were taken seriously. With Lady Gregory, he founded the national theatre and unearthed two dramatists of genius in Synge and O'Casey. He was a voice: sometimes of conscience, sometimes of celebration, sometimes of complaint, but a voice whose rhetoric has worked itself into the consciousness of modern Ireland with a force like no other.

There were other voices in the post-Parnell ferment. One which sounded in embittered opposition to Yeats and all he stood for was that of the journalist D.P. Moran, founder and editor of *The Leader*, a waspish, vituperative paper that reflected the personality of its owner. Moran was an unapologetic sectarian ethno-nationalist. For him, Irish meant Gaelic and Catholic and that was that: no others need apply. He gave expression to the lower middle-class sense of resentment that finds enemies in intellectuals, artists, the rich, other kinds of people, eccentrics and Those Who Look Down on People Like Us. There was a lot of this kind of thing around in Edwardian Ireland—as any reader of Joyce can easily confirm—and Moran had a genius for reflecting it. He was a nationalist, but he hated the placemen and time servers in the IPP, with their publican pals and big farmer supporters (here was something that he and Yeats could agree on). He had no time for Griffith and referred to Sinn Féin as 'the Green Hungarian Band'. He invented the term Irish-Ireland and explained it in a

The joint founders of the Gaelic League, Douglas Hyde (left) and Eoin Mac Neill. Hyde went on to become first President of Ireland (1937–45). Mac Neill, a distinguished scholar, was the head of the Irish Volunteers who tried to stop the 1916 Rising and the Minister for Education in the 1920s whose political career was ended by the Boundary Commission fiasco. *Hulton Archive/Getty Images*

formula: 'the foundation of Ireland is the Gael, and the Gael must be the element that absorbs.'

All the groups and tendencies whose affairs we have been reviewing were either overtly or implicitly nationalist. All seemed relatively unimportant at the time, yet within a decade had assumed positions of central importance as the Irish Revolution subverted the mental assumptions of Edwardian Ireland. We now turn to the most important of all such groups.

———

Of all the forces of internal opposition within the nationalist tent, the most potent was the Fenians, otherwise the Irish Republican Brotherhood (IRB). Founded in Dublin and New York in 1858, it was a secret revolutionary conspiracy dedicated to one cause only: the destruction of British power in Ireland by force of arms.

It therefore had no truck, or very little, with parliamentary politics or the high command of the Catholic Church. The IPP and the bishops had an understanding since Parnell's time: that the bishops would throw their huge moral weight behind the Party in return for the Party seeing to Catholic educational interests at Westminster. That was precisely the problem for the IRB, this joint focus on Westminster. Nevertheless, they bent a bit from time to time, most notably in the late 1870s when the American Fenians reached a compact with Parnell and Michael Davitt, the leader of the Land

League. But ordinarily, the IRB resented incremental politics as a distraction from the holy grail of revolutionary nationalism.

It was distinctive in its social composition. From the early days, its appeal lay disproportionately with educated and self-improving town dwellers: clerks, journalists and such like. In many ways, they were the most admirable and remarkable people of their generation. The Fenians were interested in ideas. They survived various fiascos down the years, not least the abortive Rising of 1867 (an effort scarcely more glorious than that in 1848) and the terrorist dynamite campaign in Britain in the 1880s. They operated a kind of proto-democracy below the radar of the IPP and the British security services alike. While it was easy to caricature the IRB as a one-dimensional terrorist, militant organisation, knowledgeable people realised that this was far less than the truth. The Fenians were a ubiquitous presence in Ireland from their foundation. They contained many tendencies. They had contacts with all the other players in the great game down the years: Parnell may have been a member; Yeats certainly was for a while; even Griffith. The Fenians were a moral pole, thus explaining John O'Leary's otherwise gnomic utterance to Yeats that 'in this country, a man must have either the bishops or the Fenians on his side'. Parnell had their trust and at the time of the split, they supported him to a man. Redmond never had it and never understood them. When Tom Clarke, having spent fifteen years in British jails for his part in the dynamite campaign of the 1880s, was finally released he was awarded the Freedom of the City of Limerick. (Clarke had no Limerick connections.) You don't have to admire the dynamite campaign to appreciate the moral capital that Clarke was seen to possess by many nationalists.

The IRB was well embedded in the trade union movement and most of all in the early GAA. The Gaelic Athletic Association, later to become the most successful and enduring popular movement in nationalist Ireland, was under Fenian control from the start. It was precisely the sort of people who joined trades councils or founded voluntary sports clubs who were most likely to be attracted to the Fenians. Allied to the militant politics was a visceral distaste for the clericalism and clientelism of the IPP, the contempt of the idealist for the shabby provisional morality of the opportunist. It was this sense of disgust that prompted Yeats, the old Fenian, to write 'September 1913' at the time of the Lockout, a poem dripping with contempt for the piety and cupidity of the comfortable classes.

None the less, by the first decade of the twentieth century the IRB had a shopworn look. In half a century, it had achieved next to nothing beyond moral influence in its own community. Politically, the juggernaut of the bishops and the IPP was sweeping all before it, still exercising a total hegemony on the formal politics of nationalist Ireland. And yet… an entire generation, one better educated and more sceptical than before, had grown up with the feeling that there was more to life than the Irish Parliamentary Party. Something was not quite right.

Younger men like Bulmer Hobson and Denis McCullough, both of whom had been involved with Griffith and Sinn Féin, were instrumental in reviving the IRB. On New Year's Day 1907, Tom Clarke returned from America where he had spent the previous nine years. This trio, together with Sean Mac Diarmada, were the architects of the IRB revival. Clarke was an unrepentant militant Fenian and his tobacconist's shop in Parnell Street, Dublin, became the nerve centre of the revival.

It was not dramatic and it needed a moment. The moment did not come until 1 November 1913. On that date, in *An Claidheamh Soluis* (The Sword of Light), the official paper of the Gaelic League, Eoin Mac Neill published an article entitled 'The North Began', in which he praised the formation of the UVF and called on nationalists to form their own militia. This was accomplished on the 25th of the same month, when the Irish Volunteers were formed in Dublin. Mac Neill's article was either naïve or wilfully blind, for rejoicing in the formation of an armed militia bent upon the destruction of nationalism seemed an odd thing for an 'advanced' nationalist to do. At any rate, the Volunteers proved an ideal ground for IRB infiltration. By May 1914, the Volunteers numbered 80,000.

Redmond and the IPP were at this point in the throes of seeing the Home Rule Bill through parliament. Fearing a militia on his flank that was outside his control, he peremptorily demanded and got control of its executive. Then in July 1914, the Volunteers managed to land arms at Howth, on the north of Dublin Bay. After numerous unsuccessful attempts to frustrate the landing, British troops were jeered in the streets of central Dublin on their way back to barracks. They opened fire, killing three people. The contrast with Larne was total.

The North had begun all right. Mac Neill was correct in one respect: what the UVF had started was the re-militarisation of Irish politics. The parliamentary template which had largely sustained Irish public life since O'Connell's time was about to be subverted. For the first time since the 1790s, arms were to be a crucial factor. They would prove to be a dominant element in the next ten years, and without them there would have been no Irish Revolution.

———

The Home Rule Act 1914 was finally passed into law in September 1914, by which time the United Kingdom was at war. The Act was suspended for the duration of the war. John Redmond and the other leaders of the IPP waited to inherit the earth. But all was to be changed utterly. The greatest European war in history left nothing and nowhere untouched. And in Ireland, a new generation with a new cultural politics that transcended mere home rule awaited its chance.

03 | THE RISING AND THE WAR

The war that broke out in Europe in August 1914 destroyed the world of bourgeois optimism. The age of progress yielded to thirty years of slaughter. Not until the Götterdämmerung of 1945 was spent did Europe return to full secular normality.

The outbreak of war left Redmond with a tactical dilemma. His Liberal allies had delivered home rule. Nationalist Ireland had got more or less what it had been asking for in constitutional terms since Parnell's day. Its place within the United Kingdom was now established on terms for which nationalists had fought for a generation. The IPP commanded the substantial support of the electors of nationalist Ireland. The internal opposition within nationalism—the Fenians, Sinn Féin, Moran and all the rest—might grumble that it was a paltry measure, that the Irish parliament to come was little more than a glorified county council, that effective fiscal control would remain at Westminster, but in his hour of triumph Redmond could discount them. The ease with which he grabbed control of the Volunteers was evidence of his confident command. He felt in all honour that Ireland must now throw its support unequivocally behind the war effort.

On the other hand, there was a persistent strain in Irish nationalism which held that Britain's difficulty was Ireland's opportunity. British government in Ireland had always been of dubious legitimacy. The Fenian tradition, although formally weak in numbers, represented a living sensibility. The ferocity of Irish nationalist opposition to the Boer War, only fifteen years earlier, had owed everything to this tradition, and the IPP had traditionally excoriated the British Army and what they regarded as its imperial thuggery. That said, the Irish regiments of the same army were responsible for much of the thuggery: the Dublin Fusiliers, the Munster Fusiliers, the Connaught Rangers and the Inniskilling Fusiliers were a source of pride in Ireland—as well, perhaps, of a certain unstated shame. The relationship between nationalist Ireland and the British Army was not simple.

On the day the war broke out, Redmond pledged Ireland's support in the Commons by offering the Volunteers for coastal defence in Ireland, tendentiously coupling them with the UVF—in the manner of Eoin Mac Neill—by stating: 'with our brethren in the North, we will ourselves defend the coasts of our country'. The fact that

Soldiers of the Royal Irish Rifles at the Battle of the Somme. *Imperial War Museum*

his brethren in the North would not give him daylight seemed not to register with him. From the start, his ally Dillon—whose instincts were always more radical—was uneasy with Redmond's too-ready endorsement of the war effort. Redmond's next *démarche*, however, went far beyond coastal defence. Addressing the East Wicklow Volunteers in September at Woodenbridge, he called on them 'to account for yourselves as men, not only in Ireland itself, but wherever the firing line extends, in defence of right and freedom and religion in this war'. This was an open invitation to recruit, a call beyond anything that any nationalist leader might have even contemplated in the past.

What was Redmond up to? Was he simply a naïf, a decent man overwhelmed by a sense of honourable obligation in the wake of the Home Rule Act? Was he already dreaming of a separate Irish Brigade within the national army of the newly federated United Kingdom? If the latter, he got the back of the War Office's hand. Kitchener, the head of the War Office, was a Tory ultra with no liking for Irish nationalism. The two Irish Volunteer divisions of the British Army raised in the early days of the war, the 10th and 16th—these in addition to the traditional Irish regiments—were granted no official recognition as distinct entities. They were allowed no insignia that testified to their provenance. All this was in sharp contrast to the indulgence shown to the UVF, who were incorporated as coherent battalions into the new 36th (Ulster) Division, complete with insignia barely differentiated from their old UVF emblem.

This British indifference to nationalist Ireland was underscored at Westminster. A de facto coalition government of Liberals and Tories was formed to set aside partisan differences for the duration of the war. The arrangement was formalised in 1915. This immediately subverted Redmond's parliamentary traction: the Liberals no longer needed him. None the less, when the coalition was formed, Redmond was offered a cabinet seat. He declined, although it would have been more logical for him to accept—even with all the risks attendant. He strained at the gnat of a cabinet seat, having just swallowed the camel of full support for the war effort. To make matters worse, Carson's serially illegal antics in Ulster over the preceding years were rewarded with the job of attorney-general, no less. The impresario of treason was now the government's chief law officer! Carson was a big player in the Tory party, which accounted for his appointment. But the sight of him at the cabinet table while the leader of the Irish nation was outside the door seemed to speak volumes about British attitudes and priorities.

Redmond's call to arms split the Volunteers. The overwhelming majority, about 160,000 men, followed Redmond and reconstituted themselves as the National Volunteers. The minority, who retained the name of the Irish Volunteers, numbered barely 12,000. In the course of the war, about 35,000 Irishmen were to die. The best of the National Volunteers went to the front, leaving only the dead wood at home. Meanwhile, the Irish Volunteers, although small in number, were full of vitality.

Redmond had a further problem. With home rule on the statute book, what was the IPP for any more? Those nationalists opposed to the IPP, most of them identifying with or in actual membership of the Irish Volunteers, might not agree on every detail of policy, but all were agreed on some assertion of nationality well beyond what they perceived as the timidity of mere home rule. The IPP did not implode—it would be wrong to read backwards from its annihilation in 1918 in a schematic manner. It continued to perform well in the polls into 1917, but its hegemonic position was under increasing challenge from the moment of the Volunteer split.

Redmond, like everyone else, had expected a short war. His policy was based on that assumption and it was vulnerable to the hideous casualty rates steadily accumulating on the Western Front. As the war dragged on past that first Christmas—by when it was all supposed to have been over—he was ever more vulnerable to the charge that he had betrayed the Irish people, that he had become a mere recruiting sergeant for the slaughterhouse in a war which affected no vital Irish national interest.

———

From this point on until the Easter Rising, we need to keep three groups in mind. The first is the Irish Volunteers, now under the formal leadership of Eoin

The Pearse brothers, Willie (left) and Patrick. Both were executed following the 1916 Rising. Patrick achieved the iconic status of a secular saint in independent Ireland. *Topfoto*

Mac Neill. These were the minority who refused to endorse Redmond's support for the British war effort. Their position was one in which military action against the British could take place as an act of self-defence, in practice in opposition to any threat of conscription. The second group were the IRB, now recovered in strength thanks to the efforts of Bulmer Hobson and others. They were dedicated to the old Fenian ideal of a rising against British rule while the British Army was preoccupied on the Western Front. But crucially, they argued that the IRB's own constitution demanded that any such rising must command popular support. Hobson was adamant on this point. Quite how that support could be ascertained and measured was not made clear.

No such scruple inhibited the third group. This was a secret subset of the IRB, the self-styled Military Council, including Tom Clarke, Sean Mac Diarmada and Padraig Pearse. They were for a rising regardless of public support. It was they who organised the Easter Rising of 1916. The Rising was, therefore, the work of a secret minority within a minority of a minority.

This group made one important alliance in January 1916. James Connolly's Irish Citizen Army had originally been formed to protect workers from police brutality during the 1913 Lockout. When the dispute ended, the ICA gradually atrophied and by early 1916 had barely 200 members. They were well trained and they had arms. Connolly had been disgusted by the failure of international socialism to stop the war. This, combined with his hatred of what he called the Brigand Empire, impelled him towards a specifically Irish revolution. None the less, it is impossible to know whether his threat to go ahead with a military rising of his own was simply bluff or whether he was in earnest. At any event, he did much to dispel any doubts among members of the Military Council. The rising was set for Easter Sunday 1916.

Why Easter? The symbolic Christian moment of re-birth, the ultimate renewal, is the most plausible possibility. Ireland was a country suffused in religious sentiment, even by contemporary standards. Pearse certainly had a mystical streak to him, as his verse demonstrates. But mysticism was no good without arms, and in this pursuit the Military Council used the services of Sir Roger Casement to purchase weapons from the Germans.

Casement was a distinguished exotic. Born in Dublin and raised in Co. Antrim, he came from a well-to-do Protestant family. He entered the British colonial service in Africa and distinguished himself by exposing the gross humanitarian abuses committed by Belgian employers and administrators in the Congo. He subsequently exposed similar abuses in Putamayo in Peru. He received his knighthood in 1911 and retired from the foreign service two years later, filled with a disgust for imperialism in general, not excluding British imperialism. His status as outsider was compounded by his homosexuality. His anti-imperialism brought him into the ambit of Irish nationalist circles. He had been a member of the Gaelic League since 1904 and was a friend of Bulmer Hobson. He joined the Volunteers in 1913. At the start of the war, he was in Germany trying to enlist Volunteers among captured Irish prisoners. He persuaded the Germans to furnish him with arms for the proposed rising but feeling that the response was niggardly—they only offered 20,000 guns—he sailed for Ireland with the intention of doing what he could to call the whole thing off.

Casement was captured off the coast of Co. Kerry. The boat with the guns was scuttled by its skipper and the arms went to Davy Jones's Locker. The Dublin Castle authorities, who had suspected that something was up but were not sure what, now assumed that whatever danger there was had passed. One could hardly blame them in the circumstances, although it must be noted that a softening of the traditionally tough intelligence system since the Liberals had returned to office in 1906 had given the Military Council a breathing space they might not have enjoyed in earlier times.

The Castle authorities were not the only ones surprised. The formal leaders of the Irish Volunteers, under whose umbrella the Rising was to take place, realised that they had been hoodwinked. Pearse had a pained conversation with Eoin Mac Neill in which he told him bluntly: 'We have used your name and influence for what they are worth but we have done with you now.' Likewise, those on the Supreme Council of the IRB—Hobson et al—who were not privy to the conspiracy. The Volunteers had been parading around Dublin and other towns at weekends for many months past and had

A poster that symbolised Unionist Ulster's defiance following the Larne gun-running. *Corbis/Michael Nicholson*

TWO MINDS WITH BUT A SINGLE THOUGHT — NOW!

A highly fanciful cartoon postcard showing Redmond and Carson arm-in-arm on the outbreak of the Great War. In fact, it was never so, except in the optimistic imagination of the English cartoonist. *Mary Evans Picture Library*

From the start of the war, the British Army used every possible means of persuasion to generate recruits for the Irish regiments. *National Library of Ireland*

A scarf containing the words and music to 'It's a long way to Tipperary'. *The Art Archive/Eileen Tweedy*

Two flags replaced the Union Jack on top of the GPO during Easter Week. One was the Tricolour, the other was this. *Topfoto*

The cover of a special edition of *Irish Life* on the events of the Rising. *Mary Evans Picture Library*

A painting in the heroic style by Thomas Ryan, RHA, showing Volunteers in the GPO during Easter Week. *Thomas Ryan, RHA*

In order to prevent further slaughter of the civil population and in the hope of saving the lives of our followers, the members of the Provisional Government present at Headquarters have decided on an unconditional surrender, and Commandant or officers commanding districts will order their commands to lay down arms.

P. H. Pearse

Dublin.
30th April 1916.

Pearse's surrender note.

The spot in the stonebreaker's yard at Kilmainham Jail where the 1916 leaders were executed. *Irish Times*

Irish nationalism was taking on the greatest power in the contemporary world, as this map of the British Empire from just before the First World War demonstrates.

A French postcard showing a waspish de Valera stinging Lloyd George. *Mary Evans Picture Library*

An illustration from
an Italian newspaper
showing the IRA raid
on a troop train at
Upton Station, Co.
Cork. *Mary Evans
Picture Library*

A view of rioters
looting a licensed
premises during
street fighting in
Belfast. The police
can be seen
advancing in the
background. *Mary
Evans Picture
Library*

Sir Roger Casement, diplomat, humanitarian, nationalist. *National Library of Ireland*

been regarded by the authorities and the populace alike as a bit of a joke. The manoeuvres scheduled for Easter Sunday were to be the cloak for the Rising.

Mac Neill promptly ordered the cancellation of all Volunteer manoeuvres for Easter Sunday and saw to it that copies of the order were delivered by car to provincial outposts. The result was that the Rising, when it did break out on the Monday—one day late—was an affair almost completely confined to Dublin.

———

On Easter Monday, 24 April 1916, at 11.50 a.m., Arthur Hamilton Norway, the head of the Irish Post Office service, left the General Post Office in Sackville Street (now O'Connell Street) to walk across the river to Dublin Castle. He was to meet Major Ivor Price, the head of army intelligence in Ireland, and Sir Matthew Nathan, the under-secretary for Ireland, who was head of the civil service. Shortly after Norway began his stroll, a group of about 150 armed men formed ranks outside Liberty Hall in Beresford Place. They marched along Abbey Street and debouched into Sackville Street, where they halted opposite the GPO, then and now the most imposing building in the street.

Some wore Volunteer uniforms, some the uniform of the Irish Citizen Army, some no uniforms at all. Their armaments were rudimentary, a mixture of shotguns, rifles and handguns. Sackville Street was relatively empty: it was a public holiday. Thirty miles north-west of the city the Irish Grand National was being run at Fairyhouse race course (an Easter Monday tradition that happily endures to this day).

The few people who observed these armed men might have supposed them to be yet another group playing toy soldiers, as so many had been doing for months past. Their illusions were suddenly dispelled when Connolly barked forth the order: 'The GPO—charge!' The element of surprise was total. The armed guards protecting the GPO were overwhelmed, although they would have been anyway. They had no ammunition for their guns!

Once established inside the post office, the insurgents struck the Union flag and ran up two flags in its place. The first was a plain green flag with the words 'Irish Republic' written on it. The other was the green, white and orange tricolour. Tricolour flags had become popular throughout Europe from the 1830s on, in imitation of the French republican *tricoleur*. The Irish tricolour dated from the days of the Young Irelanders in the 1840s and had been associated ever since with advanced nationalism. This was the first time it had ever flown over a public building in Ireland.

With that, Padraig Pearse stepped out of the GPO and stood under the great portico in Sackville Street. He read the following document to a bemused, if not actually amused, gathering of the populace.

POBLACHT NA H EIREANN

THE PROVISIONAL GOVERNMENT
OF THE
IRISH REPUBLIC
TO THE PEOPLE OF IRELAND

IRISHMEN AND IRISHWOMEN: In the name of God and of the dead generations from which she receives her old tradition of nationhood, Ireland, through us, summons her children to her flag and strikes for her freedom.

Having organised and trained her manhood through her secret revolutionary organisation, the Irish Republican Brotherhood, and through her open military organisations, the Irish Volunteers and the Irish Citizen Army, having patiently perfected her discipline, having resolutely waited for the right moment to reveal itself, she now seizes that moment, and, supported by her exiled children in America and by gallant allies in Europe, but relying in the first on her own strength, she strikes in full confidence of victory.

We declare the right of the people of Ireland to the ownership of Ireland, and to the unfettered control of Irish destinies, to be sovereign and indefeasible. The long usurpation of that right by a foreign people and government has not extinguished the right, nor can it ever be extinguished except by the destruction of the Irish people. In every generation the Irish people

Lower Sackville (O'Connell) Street and Eden Quay at the end of Easter Week. *Camera Press*

have asserted their right to national freedom and sovereignty; six times during the last three hundred years they have asserted it to arms. Standing on that fundamental right and again asserting it in arms in the face of the world, we hereby proclaim the Irish Republic as a Sovereign Independent State, and we pledge our lives and the lives of our comrades-in-arms to the cause of its freedom, of its welfare, and of its exaltation among the nations.

The Irish Republic is entitled to, and hereby claims, the allegiance of every Irishman and Irishwoman. The Republic guarantees religious and civil liberty, equal rights and equal opportunities to all its citizens, and declares its resolve to pursue the happiness and prosperity of the whole nation and all of its parts, cherishing all of the children of the nation equally and oblivious of the differences carefully fostered by an alien government, which have divided a minority from the majority in the past.

Until our arms have brought the opportune moment for the establishment of a permanent National, representative of the whole people of Ireland and elected by the suffrages of all her men and women, the Provisional Government, hereby constituted, will administer the civil and military affairs of the Republic in trust for the people.

We place the cause of the Irish Republic under the protection of the Most High God. Whose blessing we invoke upon our arms, and we pray that no one who serves that cause will dishonour it by cowardice, in humanity, or rapine. In this supreme hour the Irish nation must, by its valour and discipline and by the readiness of its children to sacrifice themselves for the common good, prove itself worthy of the august destiny to which it is called.

Signed on Behalf of the Provisional Government.
Thomas J. Clarke,
Sean Mac Diarmada, Thomas MacDonagh,
P. H. Pearse, Eamonn Ceannt,
James Connolly, Joseph Plunkett

The garrison set about sandbagging the building against the anticipated British counter-attack. Sniper posts were established nearby and side streets were barricaded.

Other rebel positions were established around the city at the Four Courts, the Mendicity Institute, Jameson's Distillery, Jacob's biscuit factory, Boland's Mills, the South Dublin Union and St Stephen's Green. The latter group actually dug themselves into trenches, in the manner of the Western Front, in the public park itself. Under British artillery and rifle assault, they were forced to retreat to the relative safety of the College of Surgeons on the west side of the Green, which they held for the rest of the week.

The first proper military action of the Easter Rising took place at Dublin Castle. For centuries, it had been the cortex of English power in Ireland. Its symbolic power, in the eyes of Irish nationalists, was potent. Yet on Easter Monday 1916, it lay practically undefended. It was attacked by members of the Irish Citizen Army

under the command of Captain Sean Connolly (un-
related to James). Norway was in the building, having
his meeting with Price and Nathan. Shortly after
midday, they heard what was the first shot of the 1916
Rising being fired at the gate of the Upper Castle Yard.

The shot had killed an unarmed Irishman, the sole
member of the Dublin Metropolitan Police at the gate.
Constable James O'Brien had been shot through the
head. Pressing on to the guardroom, the Citizen Army
men came upon six British soldiers preparing their
lunch. They quickly forced them to surrender—and
then did nothing. They seemed not to realise that those
six troops comprised the entire defensive capability of
the nerve centre of British power in Ireland. The Castle
was theirs for the taking and they would have got Major
Price and Sir Matthew Nathan, not to mention Mr
Norway, as an unsolicited bonus. But instead they
did nothing at all. True, the Castle would have been
impossible to hold against a determined British counter-
attack, which was certain to come. Also, the sheer
reputation of the Castle as an impregnable fortress was
intimidating, if a long way short of reality. Most of all,
they probably assumed that there simply had to be substantial numbers of troops in the complex and that a
counter-attack was imminent. In fact, there was a total
of only two officers and twenty-five men at the far side
of the Castle complex. That was all.

Instead, Sean Connolly ordered his men to fall back to
the nearby City Hall, thus missing what would have
been one of the most spectacular *coups de theatre* in

The men of Easter Week. Volunteers in the GPO garrison (from left): Des O'Reilly, T. Nolan, P. Byrne, Jack Doyle, Tom McGrath, Hugh Thornton, P. Twamley, unknown. *Kilmainham Gaol Collection*

Irish history. The whole Rising was a piece of theatre, the symbolic display of an alternative politics. It seemed a pity that its supreme moment of dramatic possibility was so casually tossed away. City Hall and a couple of outlying rebel positions associated with it in Dame Street lasted barely twenty-four hours in ICA hands before the British re-captured them. In the meantime, Sean Connolly was killed.

On the Tuesday, the British moved troops of the 25th Irish Reserve Infantry Brigade up from the Curragh under the command of General W.H.M. Lowe. Arriving at Kingsbridge (now Heuston) station, they began to throw a cordon around the city centre such as would trap most of the rebel positions within. The southern leg of the cordon was intended to run along the south quays at Usher's Island, which brought the British into a firefight with Sean Heuston's outpost at the Mendicity Institute that was not resolved for three days. In St Stephen's Green, the British occupied the Shelbourne Hotel in the small hours of the morning and had machine-gun emplacements on the upper floors with a clear field of fire across to Surgeons.

On Wednesday, with Lowe's 5,000 troops completing the encircling cordon, the gunboat *Helga* sailed up the Liffey and tied up at George's Quay across from Liberty Hall. At 8 a.m., believing Liberty Hall still to be full of rebels and the nerve centre of the rebellion, it fired a shell at the building. The alignment of the gun was wrong, however, and the shell hit the Loop Line railway bridge—a candidate for the ugliest structure in the city—with a clatter that was heard all over the city centre. The gun was adjusted and the next shell cleared the bridge and and made ribbons of Liberty Hall. The rebel nest contained no one more threatening to imperial security than the caretaker, Peter Ennis, who promptly took off for his life up Eden Quay pursued by a hail of machine-gun bullets. He made it.

Not everyone was so lucky. Two hours later, three men were shot in cold blood in Portobello Barracks, Rathmines. They had been arrested the night before. They were Francis Sheehy-Skeffington and two loyalist journalists, MacIntyre and Dickson. 'Skeffy' was one of the best-known and gifted eccentrics in a city with no shortage of them. He was a noisy campaigner for voting rights for women, a pacifist and vegetarian. He had been arrested in the act of trying to prevent looting. These three unfortunates were placed in the care of a deranged officer called Captain J.C. Bowen-Colthurst, who after a night of prayer and self-examination, decided to execute all three. This he accomplished just after 10 a.m. on Wednesday morning. Three more innocent people in all of Dublin it would have been impossible to find.

The *Helga*, meanwhile, having disposed of Liberty Hall, steamed a little bit downriver and began to shell the rear of the Boland's Mills garrison. In fact, the garrison commander had flown a rebel flag from a disused and unoccupied building nearby and the *Helga* blazed away uselessly at this, leaving the main garrison unscathed. The commander's name was Éamon de Valera, son of a Cuban-Spanish father and an Irish mother, giving the

first evidence of a craftiness that would sustain him
through an Irish political career of more than half a
century.

It was a genuine outpost of Boland's Mills, in a tall
house commandeered by Volunteers at Mount Street
Bridge, where the British suffered the heaviest casualties
of the entire Rising. On Wednesday afternoon, the
British landed a large body of troops at Kingstown (now
Dun Laoghaire) and marched them into town intending
to quarter them in various barracks. Their marching
route brought them along Northumberland Road and
straight on to the crossing of the Grand Canal at Lower
Mount Street. Here, twelve Volunteers pinned them
down from noon until dusk. The British lost over 200
men. Four of the Volunteers survived.

By Wednesday evening, the British were deploying
artillery against the GPO. On Thursday, the whole of
Lower Sackville Street was ablaze. In the post office,
Connolly was the man in charge. But on Thursday afternoon, he sustained a serious wound and was severely
incapacitated thereafter. The other leaders were ineffec-
tual. Pearse was a propagandist, not a soldier. Clarke and
Mac Diarmada were conspirators and had set everything up for the Rising, but they had no military capacity. Plunkett, who had drafted the strategic plan for the
Volunteers, was in the last throes of tuberculosis.

On Friday, General Sir John Maxwell arrived from
England to assume supreme command of British troops
in Ireland. By mid-afternoon the roof of the GPO was
ablaze. At six, there occurred one of the most poignant

James Connolly, leader of the Irish Citizen Army and military commander during the 1916 Rising. *RTÉ Stills Library*

deaths of the Rising. M.J. O'Rahilly, self-styled 'The O'Rahilly', a founder-member of the Volunteers, had been an ally of Bulmer Hobson's in opposing the Rising and had even used his car to drive around the country on the previous weekend to deliver Mac Neill's counter-manding order to provincial units. He was astonished to discover on returning to Dublin that the Rising was on after all. Feeling it his duty to do so, he joined the GPO garrison. Now, on the Friday afternoon he led a break-out from the burning post office and died at the head of his little platoon in nearby Moore Lane. Yeats immortalised him:

> 'Am I such a craven that
> I should not get the word
> But for what some travelling man
> Had heard I had not heard?'
> Then on Pearse and Connolly
> He fixed a bitter look:
> 'Because I helped to wind the clock
> I come to hear it strike.'

Later that evening and into the early hours of Saturday, the last major action of the Rising took place in nearby North King Street. The rebels were well dug in here, their position centred on an abandoned pub still referred to by old-timers in Dublin as Reilly's Fort. The troops sent to take this position frontally were tough men of the South Staffordshire Regiment and they had been among those who had taken a mauling at Mount

Surrender: On the Saturday of the Rising Patrick Pearse, as commander of Volunteer forces in the GPO garrison, surrenders to Brigadier-General Lowe at the junction of Moore Lane and Parnell Street. RTÉ *Stills Library*

Street Bridge on the Wednesday. They hated this guerrilla warfare in a strange city where the enemy did not always wear uniform and the civilian population were treacherous. It took until 9 a.m. on Saturday to dislodge the little garrison, but in the meantime some of the South Staffs had cracked and taken it out on civilians in the local tenements. Fifteen innocent men were murdered.

It ended on Saturday at 2.30 p.m. The inferno of the GPO had been abandoned. Pearse, now operating out of rebel headquarters in the back parlour of Hanlon's the fishmongers at 16 Moore Street, marched up to the nearest army position under a flag of surrender and handed his sword to General Lowe. The injured Connolly was removed to the Red Cross hospital at Dublin Castle. The rest of the Volunteers were gradually rounded up and marched off to military barracks around the city. In some of the poorer areas, they were pelted with rotten fruit and vegetables and had chamber pots emptied over them from high tenement windows. The first anniversary of the second Battle of Ypres was fast approaching, where the Dublin Fusiliers had suffered heavy casualties. There were war widows in those tenements.

The aftermath is quickly told: the courts martial; the horribly drawn-out executions, culminating in the wounded Connolly, unable to stand, being shot in an armchair; the trial and execution of Casement; the gradual but palpable change of public mood so brilliantly anticipated by James Stephens in his diary of

Easter Week: 'The truth is that Ireland is not cowed. She is excited a little.... She was not with the revolution, but in a few months she will be, and her heart which was withering will be warmed by the knowledge that men have thought her worth dying for.'

04 | FROM THE RISING TO PARTITION

Her heart which had been withering. It was a constant refrain among all who found themselves dissatisfied with the IPP and home rule, who had absorbed some or all of the intellectual, artistic and emotional ferment of the post-Parnell generation, who found the Party shifty, temporising and corrupt. Theirs was the sensibility that now began its rise to victory. It was in many respects a simple generational change, compounded by the closing of the emigration routes during the war. Many of the brightest and most enterprising, who might have taken the boat, perforce stayed at home.

But the change of mood embodied more than that. After 1916, the Fenian consciousness entered the mainstream of Irish nationalist life, moving from the marginal position it had occupied since the 1880s. It stood for something real. And that reality was the desire, long rooted in the nationalist/Catholic community, to be shot of the British. Home rule was all right when that was the best that could be had. When a glimpse of something more complete was proposed, the stakes were raised. It might be only a slight exaggeration to say that, at heart, every nationalist was a republican separatist. Certainly, as decade followed decade from the Famine to 1916, the numbers who wished for the maximum possible political distance between Britain and Ireland increased. The Irish Revolution was about the acceleration of this process under pressure of the Ulster Crisis and the Great War.

———

The change of mood anticipated by James Stephens was not long in making itself felt. Both Redmond and Dillon spoke in the House against the policy of executing the leaders of the Rising. Whatever misgivings the government may have had, they effectively left the matter to General Maxwell, the military commander on the ground in Dublin. It is all too easy to characterise Maxwell as a standard-issue military dolt, indifferent to the nuances of politics. His imposition of martial law and his policy of executing the leaders of the Rising were certainly politically inept, but from a soldier's perspective they made perfect sense. The rebels had invoked the assistance of Britain's principal enemy in the middle of the biggest war of modern times, this at a moment when the struggle at the front was at a desperate and uncertain stage. He may have considered that the political re-percussions were nothing to do with him. But they certainly had to do with the government. And the government supported him.

Dillon, in particular, understood the effect that the executions might have on nationalist public opinion. His condemnation of the policy in the Commons was especially robust. He told the House that 'it would have been a damned good thing for you if your soldiers were able to put up as good a fight as did these men in Dublin'. Suddenly, for Dillon at least, the army on the Western Front was 'your army'. So who constituted 'our army' in Dillon's eyes? And were not the IPP horribly compromised by their pro-recruiting calls for 'your army' over the previous two years?

At least as significant as Dillon's outburst was the response of Bishop Edward O'Dwyer of Limerick to General Maxwell. The general had requested the bishop to discipline two of his priests who had publicly expressed republican views. The bishop let Maxwell have it: 'You took good care that no plea for mercy should interpose on behalf of the poor young fellows who surrendered to you in Dublin.... Personally, I regard your action with horror and I believe that it has outraged the conscience of the country.' The bishops and the Party had been like an arse and a shirt since the 1880s. O'Dwyer's robust language was the first sign of a shift in episcopal support from the IPP to Sinn Féin, which was to be complete by 1918.

The Prime Minister, H.H. Asquith (centre) arrives in Dublin in the aftermath of the Rising. *The Illustrated London News Picture Library*

The IPP did not implode immediately. It continued to win by-elections in the period after the Rising. But it also began to lose them, as a new force began to take shape. The original Sinn Féin had been part of the nationalist fringe in the era prior to the Rising: the name had denoted a mood as much as a series of policies. Insofar as the policies themselves went, they included a monarchist constitutional arrangement along Habsburg lines. Yet the name Sinn Féin came to be a shorthand for all the radical nationalist movements, including the republicans. The British insisted on referring to Easter Week as the Sinn Féin Rebellion, although Sinn Féin had nothing whatever to do with it.

It meant that when all those broadly sympathetic to the Rising, or at least disenchanted with the IPP, began to coalesce politically in the aftermath of Easter Week, Sinn Féin was the name they adopted. This led to a fundamental transformation in the movement. No longer a fringe outfit, it now began to challenge the IPP for primacy in nationalist Ireland. It did this by developing into what the IPP had long been: a coalition of interests. It was not an out-and-out republican party, although it certainly contained many principled republicans.

Its first success came in the North Roscommon by-election of February 1917. The IPP candidate was opposed by Count George Noble Plunkett, the father of Joseph Plunkett, one of the executed leaders of the Rising. (His title was of papal provenance.) He was not an official Sinn Féin candidate but he did have Sinn Féin support. He won by 3,022 votes to 1,708 for the Party man. He was an interesting example of the radicalisation of nationalist opinion. He himself was no fire-breathing radical. On the contrary, he had been a conventional Parnellite in the 1890s, with one unsuccessful Westminster campaign behind him. As recently as 1914, he had applied unsuccessfully for the position of Under-Secretary for Ireland, which would have made him the country's chief civil servant in charge of the Castle administration.

In May, Sinn Féin repeated its success in another by-election in nearby South Longford when Joseph McGuinness of Sinn Féin squeaked a victory over the IPP candidate by 32 votes out of nearly 3,000. At the time, the new MP was sequestered in Lewes jail at His Majesty's Pleasure and Sinn Féin—which was to prove fertile in the coining of catchy political slogans—urged the voters to 'put him in to get him out'. Then, in July, the most senior surviving garrison commandant from the Rising won the East Clare by-election for Sinn Féin: his name was Éamon de Valera. Two days after his victory, he declared bluntly: 'If Ulster stands in the way of the attainment of Irish freedom, Ulster should be coerced.' He did not say how.

These events were straws in the wind, but not decisive in themselves. At the same time, 'normal' politics continued. In mid-1916 Lloyd George sold the Ulster Unionists a proposal for home rule with permanent exclusion for Ulster. He then sold a similar proposal to Redmond, but with only temporary exclusion until the end of the war. The southern unionists rejected any concession of home rule, but the Ulster Unionist Council accepted a permanent six-county exclusion. Redmond and Dillon bullied a convention of northern nationalists into accepting a temporary exclusion proposal.

In the middle of this farrago of prevarication and deceit, the British Army fought the Battle of the Somme, the biggest and bloodiest battle in which it was involved in the war. The casualties on the first day were 58,000 on the British side alone, of whom 20,000 were killed outright. It was the bloodiest day in the long history of the British Army. The Somme offensive lasted from 1 July to 18 November before being abandoned for little or no gain. The futility of the loss of life on such an enormous scale without any decisive victory provoked a crisis in London. The Military Service Act had already introduced conscription for all of the UK except Ireland: from now on the temptation to extend conscription to Ireland grew, with fateful results.

Among the regiments that bore the brunt of losses on the Somme, none suffered more than the 36th Ulsters, the old UVF in uniform. They were given the task of attacking uphill against the heavily fortified position at Thiepval, with instructions to capture and hold an important position on the German lines known as the Schwaben Redoubt. This they did, but at a terrible cost. They suffered over 5,000 casualties on that first day, of whom 2,000 died. Further losses mounted as the battle continued. The casualty figures bear comparison with the total losses in the Easter Rising (about 500 dead and

An anti-conscription rally. Nothing united different shades of Irish nationalism like the conscription issue. It also ensured the final triumph of Sinn Féin over the Irish Party. *RTÉ Stills Library*

2,500 wounded, most of them civilians), not because one is comparing like with like but because unionists inevitably made the comparison: while their men were giving their lives for king and country, disloyal rebels were stabbing them in the back. Of course, that was exactly how nationalists did not see it. In that sense, the two headline events of 1916, the Easter Rising and the Battle of the Somme, served only to deepen the alienation between the two Irish traditions: the more each side asserted its case in a fit of righteous virtue, the more remote it became from the other. This was a major problem for nationalism, arguing as it was from an assumption of insular unity.

———

Lloyd George replaced Asquith as Prime Minister in December 1916. With the war going badly, a more vigorous and bellicose administration was needed. Despite the enormous pressures on him, the new Prime Minister still needed to keep an eye on Ireland. In the course of 1917, he arranged for an Irish Convention at which all shades of political opinion (except Sinn Féin) made one final effort to find an accommodation. It failed, although it was not the outright failure that it might have been: there were some tantalising shuffles towards compromise. Overall, however, the big issues remained intractable and the well-rehearsed differences that were now hoary with repetition caused the

Convention finally to subside in the spring of 1918. It is doubtful if Lloyd George had expected it to succeed but at least it kept the Irish occupied among themselves for a while.

On the nationalist side, Sinn Féin reconstituted itself. In deference to his position as the senior survivor of the Rising, de Valera replaced Arthur Griffith as president of the party. It adopted a new constitution, enshrining its political ambiguities neatly in Article 2: 'Sinn Féin aims at securing the international recognition of Ireland as an independent Irish Republic. Having achieved that status the Irish people may by referendum freely choose their own form of government.' This masterly piece of logic-chopping was the work of de Valera, who thus managed to gather under the new Sinn Féin umbrella republicans of the Fenian tradition and other advanced nationalists whose politics were not necessarily as doctrinaire. It was the first manifestation of a serpentine political intellect that would dominate his country for half a century.

As if to symbolise the passage of nationalist political leadership to the post-Rising generation, John Redmond died in March 1918. The previous June, his brother Willie had been killed while leading the 5th Battalion of the Royal Irish Regiment at the Battle of Messines Ridge. John Dillon became the new leader of the IPP, but it was an increasingly hollow inheritance. Not only was the Party associated with the failure of yet another British constitutional initiative, the Irish Convention, it now faced the disaster of conscription. In

April 1918, reacting to renewed heavy losses on the Western Front caused by the alarming successes of the Germans' spring offensives, Lloyd George proposed enabling legislation to make it possible to extend the Military Service Act to Ireland. He had been warned time out of number that such a move would be met with universal outrage in nationalist Ireland, but given the military situation in France he could be forgiven for thinking that any expedient—however desperate—was better than military defeat. And the military situation was truly frightening: in the months of March and April 1918, the British Army lost over 300,000 men dead or wounded on the Western Front. Only a year before, Lloyd George had told the Commons that conscription in Ireland would produce barely 160,000 men, most of them at the point of a bayonet and many of them farm workers whose existing contribution to the war effort was vital. By April 1918, he was prepared to consider any option.

It was a knife in the heart for the IPP. John Dillon withdrew the Party from Westminster in protest, thereby tacitly conceding Sinn Féin's abstentionist point. The conscription threat galvanised Irish nationalists like nothing before: all shades of opinion, lay and clerical, were opposed to any such move. No more telling argument could be made for the complete collapse of British moral authority in nationalist Ireland.

The Lord Mayor of Dublin, Laurence O'Neill, organised a Mansion House Conference to build a unified nationalist platform against conscription. Dillon and de Valera

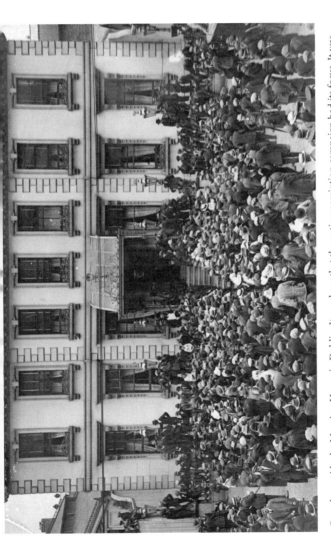

Crowds outside the Mansion House in Dublin. It was here that the anti-conscription campaign had its focus. It was also here that the First Dáil met in January 1919. *National Library of Ireland*

were there, as were dissident Nationalist MPs like Tim Healy and William O'Brien. Bitter political rivals united in a common cause, in a manner not seen since Parnell's day. An anti-conscription pledge—drafted by de Valera—was signed by almost 2 million people across the country. It was a nationalist echo of the Ulster Solemn League and Covenant. The campaign had the overt support of the Catholic hierarchy, traditionally cautious but shrewd enough to recognise the way the wind was blowing. The Irish Trade Union Congress called a general strike, which was observed everywhere except—no surprise, this—in Belfast. Irish-American organisations, traditionally of a Fenian disposition, organised rallies and raised money for the cause.

Conscription was the issue that won Ireland for advanced nationalism. It united the entire community around what was effectively a Sinn Féin agenda. The IPP was left looking like a busted flush. Recruitment to the Irish Volunteers soared. In May, the government cooked up a totally spurious 'German Plot', in which Lord French, the commander of the original British Expeditionary Force to France at the beginning of the war and now Lord Lieutenant of Ireland, concocted 'evidence' of Sinn Féin's 'treasonable communication with the German enemy'. French had been a less than stellar general and had been relieved of his command after the Battle of Loos in 1915. His performance in the political minefield that was Ireland in 1918 was as clumsy as one might have expected from a military man of unexceptional intelligence. In May, he organised the arrest of most of the Sinn Féin leadership on grounds of complicity in the German Plot. De Valera was lodged in Lincoln Jail. Naturally, this did him and the rest of the leadership no harm at all in nationalist eyes. On the contrary, it reinforced the purity of their patriotism.

Arthur Griffith was also lifted and ensconced in Gloucester prison. From there, he learned of his election as a Sinn Féin MP in the East Cavan by-election in June. This was a significant result, not just because it confirmed the flow tide for Sinn Féin but because it did so in the IPP's organisational heartland: south Ulster was the part of the country where the Party's structures had held up best against the Sinn Féin challenge.

On the very same day that Griffith was elected, the government's conscription plans were abandoned. It had taken just two months of furious agitation in Ireland to accomplish this. There were other reasons for the *volte face*. Ludendorff's offensives on the Western Front were being contained by the late spring, although they were still inflicting heavy casualties. Moreover, the United States had entered the war on the Allied side in the autumn of 1917 and by the summer of 1918 the American Expeditionary Force was being augmented to the tune of 10,000 men a day. In this light, the panic over Irish conscription seems foolish and headless. But the pressure that all Allied governments were facing— especially the British and the French—was almost intolerable. Not until August and September did the Allied counter-attacks make a decisive breach in the German ranks.

The Allies finally won the war in November, and in December there took place the 'khaki election', held on a greatly expanded franchise. It was effectively the first UK election held under universal male suffrage. Women over thirty also had the vote for the first time. The effect was to increase the size of the Irish electorate from 700,000 to 2 million. It is reasonable to suppose that this accounted in part for the triumph of Sinn Féin and the near obliteration of the IPP. The Party had won 73 seats in 1910. Now Sinn Féin had 73 out of the 105 Irish seats. The IPP was reduced to a miserable six. Of these, four were in Ulster where the Party and Sinn Féin had agreed a pact to allow the Party an unopposed run lest a split nationalist vote let a Unionist slip in. There was no doubt at all that Sinn Féin was now the undisputed political voice of nationalist Ireland.

————

True to their principles, those Sinn Féin MPs who were not in jail following the German Plot refused to take their seats at Westminster and instead constituted themselves as Dáil Éireann, the assembly of Ireland, which met for the first time at the Mansion House in Dublin on 21 January 1919. The Dáil appointed delegates to represent it at the forthcoming Paris peace talks, designed to hammer out a post-war settlement for Europe. An Irish Race Convention in Philadelphia voted for full recognition of Ireland as a separate entity at the

This nationalist postcard speaks for itself.

peace conference, a vote echoed by the US House of Representatives, much to the chagrin of President Woodrow Wilson.

On 3 February 1919, de Valera was sprung from Lincoln Jail in an audacious escape orchestrated by Harry Boland and a young man from West Cork called Michael Collins. Still not thirty, Collins had been 'out' in 1916, had been interned briefly, was secretary and later president of the Supreme Council of the IRB and a member of the executive committee of the Irish Volunteers. He was also Minister for Home Affairs in the shadow government formed by Dáil Éireann. He had contacts everywhere, and he was assiduously developing a spy network to worm its way into the British administration. Traditionally, the Dublin Castle spy system had been the rock on which Irish political conspiracies had broken. Collins was in the business of turning the tables. By the middle of 1919, he would be a household name.

In April, de Valera was elected President of Dáil Éireann and Michael Collins, by now Minister for Finance in the shadow government, began an issue of republican bonds in order to raise national funds. The issue was an astonishing success. In June, de Valera left for the United States where he was to spend the next eighteen months rallying Irish-American opinion to the republican cause and trying to mobilise its influence to guide President Wilson's policy at Paris. The former proved easy, the latter not: Wilson was an Anglophile and the British effectively vetoed any suggestion that Ireland might have separate representation at the peace conference.

In the summer of 1919 the Dáil established a series of republican courts throughout much of the south and west, which effectively replaced the crown courts as the means of settling legal disputes. They were remarkably effective and widely resorted to by people of all political sympathies. In this way, the Dáil was able to make its writ run in large parts of Ireland in defiance of the British.

How could the shadow administration in Dublin, on the run from safe house to safe house, strapped for cash, harassed by the British, pull off such an audacious coup in the countryside? The answer lay in the second half of the republican offensive. On 21 January 1919, the same day that the Dáil had met for the first time, two members of the Irish Volunteers in Co. Tipperary had shot dead two members of the Royal Irish Constabulary at Soloheadbeg. These were the first shots fired in the Irish War of Independence.

The relationship between the various strands that made up the Volunteers—or the Irish Republican Army (IRA) as they became known in the course of 1919—and Sinn Féin was an uncertain one. In theory, the IRA was the army of the Republic, under ultimate civilian control. The personification of that control was the Minister for Defence in the Dáil administration, Cathal Brugha. However, the IRA contained within it (as had the Volunteers right from the start) a significant number of IRB men, and the IRB considered itself, according to its own constitution, to be the provisional government of the Republic until a fully independent state could be established. And the head of the IRB was Collins, a swaggering, overbearing personality if ever there was one. Brugha, also a 1916 veteran and brave to a fault, naturally resented the younger man.

Moreover, what did civilian control actually mean in the context of the War of Independence? Communications between Dublin and local units of the IRA were uncertain to non-existent. The war was prosecuted by energetic local commanders who knew their own areas and were disinclined to take orders from Brugha, even if those orders could get through. The most remarkable thing about the War of Independence was how local it was, depending almost entirely on the initiative of individual commanders. A county as fiercely republican as Kerry fired few shots in anger, while the neighbouring county of Cork was a graveyard for the crown forces. Co. Longford was a hotbed of the war, largely thanks to the aggression and organisational skills of Sean Mac Eoin.

The primary target of the IRA was the police, the Royal Irish Constabulary (RIC), the local eyes and ears of British government in Ireland. Rural barracks, most of them poorly defended, were targeted and progressively abandoned by the police. Most RIC men were Irish nationalists and Catholics, but that availed them nought in the eyes of the IRA. Indeed, it compounded their treachery in their enemy's eye. From the middle of 1919, IRA killings were stepped up. District Inspector Hunt of the RIC was killed in Thurles, Co. Tipperary, in June. Detective Patrick Smith of the G Division (Special

Oliver Gogarty, who despised him, called him 'the Spanish onion in the Irish stew'. But Éamon de Valera, seen here addressing a meeting in 1917, became head of Sinn Féin after the Rising and was the political leader of Irish nationalism until the Treaty split. Thereafter, he founded Fianna Fáil and dominated politics in the Free State/Republic until the end of the 1950s. *Bettmann/Corbis*

Branch) of the Dublin Metropolitan Police was shot in July. In August, Co. Clare was a hotbed of activity. By the end of September, over 5,500 raids by the police and military on private houses had taken place. British troops sacked Patrick Street in Cork. In December, the IRA came within a whisker of assassinating French, the Lord Lieutenant. By the end of the year, there were 43,000 British Army troops in Ireland.

The new year, 1920, brought a new and sinister development. The government was faced with the fact that there was an open military revolt in Ireland; that there was a shadow government capable of raising its own funds; and that an alternative system of justice was functioning in some parts of the country. Had Ireland been a distant crown colony, it would have been a relatively simple matter to send in the army. But Ireland was not a crown colony. It was an integral part of the metropolitan United Kingdom. It was this single fact that had made the whole Irish nationalist saga so difficult for the British, compounded of course by the Ulster unionist complication. London did not simply want to throw the army at the IRA, but it definitely needed to augment its military presence. So it called its new auxiliary force a police reserve. The RIC was the principal target of the rebels, so the new force would in effect be soldiers posing as police. As if to give the game away, they were put under army control.

They started recruiting for the new reserve on 2 January and the first recruits arrived in Ireland on 25 March. They were issued with dark bottle green RIC tunics, but a shortage of trousers in the same colour meant that they had to wear British Army khaki: thus the name that has stuck to them ever since, the Black and Tans. (The reference was to a famous hunt in Co. Limerick, the Scarteen Black and Tans, whose colours were and are similar.) The Tans were stationed in areas of highest IRA activity and their reputation for unblinking reprisal and counter-terror was soon established. Most of them were veterans of the Great War, either bored or unemployed or both. Random firing at civilians and the looting and burning of towns became a commonplace.

Even more vicious than the Black and Tans were the Auxiliaries, a further force raised in the middle of the year. They were paid more than the Tans and given an even freer hand than them, which they cheerfully played. The Auxiliaries were responsible for the torture and execution of prisoners and it was they who set much of the centre of Cork city ablaze in December 1920. One of their most hated commanders, Major Arthur Percival, survived three IRA assassination attempts and lived long enough to have the honour of surrendering Singapore to the Japanese in 1941.

In all, 1920 was a year of escalating violence. In March, a magistrate, Alan Bell, was assassinated in Dublin by a group called 'the Squad' under the direction of Michael Collins. An IRA attack at Ballylanders, Co. Limerick, brought Black and Tan reprisals in Limerick city the next day. So quickly had the Black and Tans acquired a reputation for atrocity that in June—barely three months after they were first deployed—the word of their excesses had travelled as far as India, tripping off a mutiny among Irish troops there. In the midst of all this chaos, Michael Collins was able to announce that his National Loan scheme had been over-subscribed by 15 per cent.

The catalogue of violence went on. In August the IRA assassinated an RIC district inspector deep in the unionist heartland of Lurgan, Co. Antrim. DI Swanzy had been implicated in the murder in March of the Sinn Féin lord mayor of Cork, Tomás MacCurtain, who had also doubled up as head of the local IRA. A Cork coroner's jury was in no doubt on the matter, finding that 'the murder was organised and carried out by the Royal Irish Constabulary officially directed by the British government'. Few doubted the basic truth of this verdict and MacCurtain duly entered the nationalist Pantheon.

Through the autumn of 1920, the IRA campaign was stepped up, most particularly in its Munster heartland. In September, a force under the command of Liam Lynch and Ernie O'Malley captured the military barracks in Mallow, Co. Cork. The RIC barracks in Trim, Co. Meath, was captured two days later. The Black and Tans responded by sacking the town in reprisal. By October, the British government acknowledged that 675 RIC barracks had been destroyed, abandoned or damaged since the start of 1919. One hundred and seventeen RIC men were dead and 185 injured in the same period. On 24 October, MacCurtain's successor as lord mayor of Cork, Terence MacSwiney, died on

Victims of the War of Independence: a British Army cadet in the foreground. In the background, two Irish Volunteers. *Hulton Archive/Getty Images*

hunger strike in Brixton Jail, London, after seventy-four days without food. On 1 November, Kevin Barry was hanged in Dublin for his part in an IRA raid in the city. He was only eighteen, and the fact that one of the British soldiers killed in the attack was younger than him was disregarded. A ballad was written about Kevin Barry—still sung to this day—and he joined MacCurtain and MacSwiney in the Pantheon.

In early November, Sean MacEoin and his men held the town of Ballinalee, Co. Longford, for a week for the IRA. The Black and Tans burned it on recapture. On the morning of 21 November, Bloody Sunday, fourteen alleged British secret agents were murdered in their beds by Collins' Squad. In the afternoon, the Black and Tans opened fire on a crowd attending a Gaelic football match at Croke Park, Dublin, killing twelve including one player. A week later, the West Cork Brigade of the IRA under Tom Barry wiped out a party of eighteen Auxiliaries in an ambush at Kilmichael. Martial law was proclaimed throughout much of Munster and the Black and Tans and Auxiliaries between them torched much of the centre of Cork city in reprisal.

———

While all this mayhem was going on, the government made a further attempt to legislate its way out of the Irish mess. In March 1920, it introduced the Government of Ireland Bill, in effect a fourth home rule measure. It repealed the 1914 Act and proposed a partition of the island. There would be two parliaments, one in Dublin and one in Belfast for the six counties of Northern Ireland. The six counties chosen—Antrim, Down, Armagh, Derry, Tyrone and Fermanagh—represented the maximum area in which a Protestant and unionist majority could be guaranteed. The remaining three counties of the historic province of Ulster were to be left in Southern Ireland.

The legislation was passed before the end of the year. It was a dead letter in the South from the start. But it held in the North. Northern Ireland was formally established as an autonomous province within the United Kingdom in May 1921. The island was partitioned: what had been unthinkable—even for Sir Edward Carson—less than a decade earlier had come to pass.

05 | PARTITION AND THE TREATY

It is worth pausing at this point. Other events—usually the end of the civil war in the South—are more commonly seen as the appropriate moments for a chapter break. Such narratives are structured around the creation of the new Southern state, proposing a continuum from the Volunteers, through 1916 and the War of Independence, the Treaty, the tragedy of the civil war and the final establishment of the institutions of the new state. Those events that do not contribute directly to this process are of necessity marginalised. But it is also right to emphasise the state breaking aspect of the narrative: partition was as important for all that followed in the next century as anything else that happened in the Irish Revolution, and it was a profound psychological shock for contemporaries. The mental unity of the island, common to people on all sides, was now decisively broken. No matter how the republican campaign went in the South, the island of Ireland was formally divided for the first time in its history.

The new statelet, Northern Ireland, was inaugurated in May 1921, while the War of Independence was still in full swing in the South. It was the product of a legislative process that had flowed from the refusal of Sinn Féin MPs elected in 1918 to take their seats at Westminster. This meant that Irish nationalists had no input into the Government of Ireland Act 1920 which established Northern Ireland. Not only that, but Lloyd George's coalition government was dominated by Conservatives and Unionists. Craig himself was a junior minister at the Admiralty and the legislation was drafted by a committee headed by Walter Long, a former parliamentary leader of the Irish Unionists.

The result was that the Ulster Unionists were able to tailor the legislation to suit their own convenience. This they did by throwing the Southern unionists to the wolves and even abandoning the three marginal Ulster counties of Cavan, Monaghan and Donegal, whose inclusion would have left the confessional balance of the partitioned province too delicate for comfort. Instead they took as many counties as would produce a secure Unionist majority. And so Northern Ireland came to comprise the six remaining Ulster counties. Three of them had solid Protestant majorities, one a narrow Protestant majority and the remaining two—Fermanagh and Tyrone—Catholic majorities. Overall, the confessional balance was enough to ensure that 40 of the 52 MPs returned to the first session of the new regional parliament in Belfast were Unionists. Craig returned from the Admiralty in London and assumed his new role as the first Prime Minister of Northern Ireland.

This new arrangement did not go uncontested. Units such as the 4th Northern Division of the IRA under the command of Frank Aiken from South Armagh—later to be a long-serving Minister for External Affairs in Dublin—began to carry the war into the North. All Northern Catholics, whether republicans or not, were horrified by partition. Theirs was a reaction that mirrored the fear of the Protestants in a unitary home rule state: that of being held hostage to the superior numbers of the sectarian enemy.

In effect, what happened in the North from 1920 to 1922 was the sectarian civil war that had threatened in 1914 and which had been averted only by the outbreak of the Great War in Europe. By now, however, the focus had shifted. In 1914, the UVF was set to resist the state. Now the state was in the hands of those who had formed and armed the UVF, and it was nationalists who were resisting the new arrangements proposed. The war in the South was between a guerrilla army fighting in the name of a putative republic—virtually established, in the old Fenian formula—and the occupying British state. The war in the North was much more of an internal affair. It was the continuation of a nineteenth-century tradition of sectarian violence. But the violence was to attain a level not known before, as nationalists found the

Anxious crowds outside the offices of the *Belfast Telegraph* checking the lists of those killed in the 1920 riots.
Hulton-Deutsch Collection/ Corbis

political tables turned on them in the most dramatic fashion.

There were serious riots in Derry in the early part of 1920 and gradually vigilante groups of Protestants began to form in west Ulster in the course of that year. In effect, the UVF was being re-born. The abandonment of rural police stations by the police under IRA pressure added to this impulse. The Protestant marching season threw fuel on this fire: by the second half of July, Catholics were being intimidated out of their work-places in Belfast. Up to 10,000 may have suffered this fate: even if that number is an exaggeration, the reality of widespread intimidation was undeniable. Equally undeniable was the fact that the IRA, although poorly armed and outnumbered, fought a bitter guerrilla war aimed at destabilising the new state before it could get itself established.

Given the superiority of Protestant numbers and their access to arms, they were always more likely to prevail in this contest. Isolated Catholic areas came under attack from Protestant mobs, often abetted by the army and police. Craig explained to an alarmed government in London that 'the loyalists…believe that the rebel plans are definitely directed towards the establishment of a republic hostile to the British Empire' and warned that 'unless urgent action is taken, civil war on a very large scale is inevitable'. In fact, what had emerged by the last quarter of 1920 was little short of civil war.

Even before the formal inauguration of the Northern Ireland state, the government decided to raise a police reserve in the North, to be known as the Ulster Special Constabulary. It was divided into three sections, A, B and C. Of these, the B Specials became the largest and most notorious group. They were for all practical purposes the UVF in state uniforms, a Protestant militia that proved efficient at petty harassment, spying on Catholic neighbours and brutally robust methods of law enforcement.

In May 1921, King George V had come to Belfast to inaugurate the new partition parliament and had made a speech calling on all sides to start afresh and to forgive and forget. It sent a signal to the Sinn Féin leadership in the South that may have led to the Truce that followed in July. But it was words on the wind in the North. The very next day, as the king's cavalry escort was returning to Dublin by train, it was ambushed by the IRA. Four men and eighty horses died. In June, the deaths of four policemen and B Specials brought reprisals against Catholics in Belfast that left ten dead. In July, just as the Truce took hold in the South, the violence got worse in the North. Sixteen Catholics and seven Protestants died. More than 200 Catholic houses were torched. By the end of 1921, the death toll in Belfast alone was 109 for the year, in addition to the injuries, intimidations and wrecking of homes and businesses.

The Truce in the South released IRA Volunteers and arms for service in the North, thus raising the stakes further. The release of IRA prisoners under the terms of the Treaty had a similar effect. Seventy-two IRA Volunteers in Belfast were being paid a monthly stipend by the

Dublin Sinn Féin government-in-waiting. In February 1922, forty-four people died in Belfast including six Catholic children killed in a bomb attack. The number in March was sixty-one dead. In April, there were further attacks and reprisals. In one instance, the police were implicated in a revenge attack on Catholic houses in Belfast that left a man and a child dead and fifty houses destroyed. Catholics burned out in Belfast fled to Dublin in the clothes they stood up in. Craig's government was thoroughly rattled: the mayhem was a direct challenge to the new provincial government's ability to maintain order in its own back yard. Was Northern Ireland viable as an entity? The IRA were doing everything they could to wreck it, or at least to compromise its internal security so badly as to paralyse it.

Craig responded with the Special Powers Act 1922. It gave the government draconian powers of arrest, indefinite detention without trial, and summary courts that could hand down the death penalty. Liberal British opinion was horrified at what it regarded as powers of Asiatic severity. Unionist backbenchers, on the other hand, thought it too pussyfooting. One MP took the view that the Act should simply empower the Home Secretary to do whatever he liked.

The IRA response to this was to step up their campaign in west Ulster, where the local Catholic majority gave them relative safety in numbers. Protestant houses and businesses were targeted. In May 1922, the war returned to Belfast as the IRA set over forty major fires in the city. As the summer came on, things got worse. An MP was murdered. Internment without trial was introduced. Even then, it was a close-run thing. The decisive event was the civil war in the South, which broke out in earnest at the end of June. By dividing the IRA and diverting its Northern command from what had been its primary purpose, it contributed to the fizzling out of the campaign. How much of the IRA retreat was due to this and how much to the severity of Craig's response is impossible to gauge.

At any rate, by 1923 the North, like the South, was restored to a nervous peace. But there was no denying that the IRA had taken on the new government and had challenged its viability as a functioning unit. The new state was, therefore, born of a victory by the state over armed republicanism. Once again, the more vigorous the assertion of nationalist rights the more terrible the unionist response. It was a vicious three years which set the pattern of zero-sum politics in Northern Ireland for the future. Perhaps it would be more correct to say that it merely underlined the zero-sum nature of the sectarian quarrel that had been visible since the 1880s.

More people died in Northern Ireland in 1922 as a result of political violence than in most years of the post-1968 Troubles. In many respects, the violence of 1920–22 anticipated the later Troubles. The principal difference was the unbridled licence permitted to and assumed by the forces of the new state. It would have been difficult, to put it no stronger, for Catholics to accommodate themselves easily to the Protestant statelet. The circumstances of its birth made it quite impossible. Contrariwise, the province's foundation experience convinced Protestants that only the sternest, most uncompromising opposition to Catholic aspirations was appropriate. It meant that public life in Northern Ireland became a forcing house for every kind of petty-minded provincial reaction, a stagnant pool of the imagination and the intellect.

———

Meanwhile, the South went its own way. Sinn Féin ignored the Government of Ireland Act 1920. Instead, the Dáil continued to meet from time to time as circumstances and British Army surveillance allowed. At the very end of 1920, the leader of Sinn Féin, Éamon de Valera, arrived back in Ireland having spent almost eighteen months in the United States.

The War of Independence showed no sign of relenting. The first half of 1921 saw a succession of incidents, mainly concentrated south of the Dublin-Galway line. In January, the IRA in Co. Clare killed six policemen, including a district inspector, in an ambush. Major-General Philip Armstrong-Holmes, the Munster divisional commander of the RIC, met a similar fate in Co. Cork. Eleven RIC men and Black and Tans died in an ambush in Co. Limerick in February. In March, at Crossbarry, the West Cork No. 3 Brigade of the IRA took on more than a thousand troops of the Essex and

Black and Tans take time off from what they do best to pose for the camera. *Hulton Archive/Getty Images*

Hampshire regiments, inflicting 86 casualties—including 39 dead—for the loss of three dead and four wounded. There was a particularly nasty incident in May near Gort, in south Co. Galway (not far from Coole Park, seat of Lady Gregory). A priest had been murdered nearby by the Black and Tans. The IRA retaliated by raiding Ballyturrin House. A captain and a lieutenant in the 17th Lancers were killed, as was the local district inspector of the RIC. His wife, now widow, who was seven months pregnant, grabbed his revolver and held the attackers at bay until she herself was killed. A second RIC man later died of his wounds. The IRA suffered no casualties, but there were reprisals in Gort and shops and property were ransacked.

In February 1921, Brigadier-General Frank Crozier resigned his command of the Auxiliaries in despair at his inability to control his men. In March, three men, including the Sinn Féin lord mayor of Limerick, were murdered by the Black and Tans. The lord mayor, George Clancy, had been a university friend of James Joyce and was the model for the character of Madden in *Stephen Hero* and Davin in *A Portrait of the Artist as a Young Man.* He was the very model of the sort of young man drawn to Sinn Féin, a Gaelic Leaguer, a hurler and an enthusiast for national pursuits of every sort. Joyce counterpoints Clancy's earnest provincialism with his own developing cosmopolitanism: even allowing for this schematic purpose, his portrait of Clancy is one of the sharpest images we have of a middle-ranking Sinn Féin activist.

By mid-April, the British cabinet was informed that the Irish military campaign was costing the government £20 million a year. In May, de Valera met Craig at a secret location in Dublin. No progress was made. De Valera regaled Craig with a lecture on Irish history that took half an hour just to get to Brian Boru. The fact was that Sinn Féin had as little clue about the Ulster Protestants as the IPP or any preceding nationalist group had. It was a dialogue of the deaf. For nationalists, the brute reality of Protestant numbers in Ulster could be met only with rhetoric, violence and insult. No nationalist policy could reach them. Therefore the policies that were proposed, whether in 1912, 1921 or later, smacked of fantasy and heart's desire.

In May, the Dublin IRA burned the Custom House. It was the headquarters of the Local Government Board. Its offices were duly torched, but the IRA were caught by a detachment of Auxiliaries and lost over a hundred men, captured following a shoot-out. It was a disaster for the IRA, paralysing what had already turned out to be a less than vigorous campaign in the capital. Moreover, they destroyed the finest classical building in the city. The incident contributed to a widening gap between Collins and de Valera, the former with a soldier's dislike of spectacular gestures for their own sake, the latter with the politician's understanding of their symbolic value.

It was the last major incident in the War. Both sides had fought each other, if not to a standstill, at least to a stalemate. And that alone was a triumph for the republicans. A truce was agreed after a series of back channel communications with Lloyd George. It came into effect on 11 July.

———

A week later, de Valera was in London for talks with Lloyd George. The Prime Minister offered Dominion Home Rule to the South. De Valera rejected it, insisting on the recognition of the Irish Republic. The Dáil supported his position unanimously. By the end of September, a conference had been arranged for London 'with a view to ascertaining how the association of nations known as the British Empire may best be reconciled with Irish national aspirations'. This formula, with its emphasis on the imperial context, contained the seeds of a republican concession.

De Valera did not go to London this time. Instead, he sent a delegation of five headed by Arthur Griffith. The others were Michael Collins, Robert Barton, Edmund Duggan and George Gavan Duffy. Their written instructions contained a basic semantic and logical contradiction. They were granted full plenipotentiary power, subject to a requirement that they convey any prospective agreement back to Dublin for cabinet approval. Why de Valera, the Sinn Féin leader and President of the Irish Republic, did not attend the Treaty discussions has vexed the minds of historians ever since. He was the most subtle and serpentine, if exasperating, intellect on the Irish side, and

An Irish Volunteer surrenders to the Auxiliaries after the bungled attack on the Custom House in Dublin in 1921. *The Allen Library*

certainly the most skilled negotiator. The explanation usually advanced is that he knew a compromise was inevitable, that this meant something less than the full republic, and that he was the person best positioned in Dublin to sell such a deal to his own radicals.

De Valera's preferred formula was external association. This meant that Ireland would be associated with the Empire but would not be a member of it. That would mean no oath of allegiance to the king. De Valera proposed this formula as a concession to Ulster Unionist concerns 'to meet whose sentiments alone this step could be contemplated'. It is doubtful if even de Valera's naïveté concerning the Unionists extended to the idea that this would satisfy them. But he certainly advanced it as a basis for a settlement that might fall short of the simon-pure republic but would still commend itself to most republican radicals.

The problem with external association was that Lloyd George had rejected it out of hand in July. It was difficult to see how he might accept it in October, especially with his parliamentary majority depending on the Conservative Party. In addition to external association, the Irish delegation was instructed to ensure that any breakdown in the talks should come on the question of partition. The British, on the other hand, wanted any break to come on an Irish refusal to accept ultimate British sovereignty.

The early negotiations turned on these points. Griffith began by proposing a possible Ulster parliament subordinate to a sovereign parliament in Dublin, not

London. Lloyd George countered by emphasising the risks he was running: his parliamentary majority depended on Tory backwoods support in the Commons. If he failed, Bonar Law was waiting in the wings to take over as Prime Minister. Sinn Féin could expect nothing from him. Lloyd George therefore needed an answer to certain fundamentals: would Ireland accept membership of the empire and allegiance to the king? Would it provide defence facilities?

Lloyd George was a masterly negotiator, with more than a touch of controlled hysteria in his performance. Moreover, he was supported by some of the greatest heavyweights of the age: Churchill, Birkenhead and Austen Chamberlain among them. Facing him was Griffith, who did not impress him, and Collins, who impressed everybody but was still barely thirty years of age. By setting these fundamental questions, Lloyd George was able to focus the negotiation on constitutional matters rather than on partition. Once settled on that ground, the Irish found it difficult to get off it.

Lloyd George formed the view that the Irish would ultimately accept the crown in return for reunification. He may well have been right: Griffith's prescription for the original Sinn Féin had been dual monarchy, born as much as anything from a belief that no settlement that excluded the crown would be acceptable in Ulster. Indeed he told Lloyd George that 'if we came to an agreement on all other points I could recommend some form of association with the crown', which, although well short of what Lloyd George needed, was enough to alarm de Valera back in Dublin. By now, the main burden of negotiation on the Irish side was being carried by Griffith and Collins in a series of bilateral meetings with two British delegates. The idea was floated of Ulster autonomy in an independent Ireland, but an Ulster reduced in size to exclude peripheral areas of the new Northern Ireland with Catholic majorities. Griffith thought this idea had promise.

Craig did not. Arriving in London from Belfast in early November, he was horrified to discover that Northern Ireland was being used as a bargaining chip in Downing Street. He dug his toes in and refused flatly to support any change whatsoever in the arrangements so recently made for Northern Ireland. (Bear in mind that it was established less than six months at this stage.) Lloyd George pleaded with Craig, threatened to resign and generally displayed the full range of his rhetorical repertoire. Craig was unmoved and unmoveable. The Prime Minister now turned back to Griffith.

He proposed a Boundary Commission to review the Northern Ireland settlement, the clear implication being that any such commission would be bound to transfer large areas of Catholic population on the margins of Northern Ireland to the South. The consequence of this, it was suggested, would be to leave the Northern Ireland rump statelet completely unviable and oblige it in time to subside into a union with the South. Griffith and Collins believed what they wanted to believe—as with so much nationalist fantasy before and since about the North. Griffith's guarded reply was that while the

Michael Collins leaving 10 Downing Street during the treaty negotiations. *Hulton Archive/Getty Images*

proposal came from the British, not the Irish side, who would therefore not be bound by it, 'we realise its value as a tactical manoeuvre and if Lloyd George made it we would not queer his position'. Having secured this tacit concession, Lloyd George now persuaded Griffith to initial a hastily drafted document. It stated that if Ulster declined to join an all-Ireland parliament it would be necessary to revise the province's boundary by the means of a Boundary Commission.

The negotiations continued, reaching a melodramatic climax on 5 December. The Irish delegation was exhausted, not least from various to-ings and fro-ings back to Dublin to consult the Sinn Féin cabinet. De Valera was concerned that they might get neither the republic nor unity, and radicals like Cathal Brugha gave a foretaste of the bitterness that the civil war would bring within the year by making snide and wounding *ad hominem* comments about how the British had clearly 'picked their men'. On the delegation's return to London, Lloyd George's sense of theatre and timing enabled him to inject real urgency into the negotiations. He threatened a break on the question of the oath of allegiance to the crown. He threatened war. In despair, Griffith conceded that if Ulster would come in he would accept the crown. At this point, Lloyd George, like a conjurer, produced Griffith's initialled note from weeks before accepting the principle of a Boundary Commission instead of a firm requirement to coerce Ulster. He accused Griffith of reneging on his word, a charge that Griffith—prickly at the best of times—could not endure.

It was the decisive psychological moment. Lloyd George applied more time pressure, demanding that the articles of agreement be signed by 10 p.m. that night, failing which he threatened 'immediate and terrible war'. It was a masterly performance by the Prime Minister, forcing a conclusion to a negotiation that had threatened to collapse. Instead, it was the Irish delegation that collapsed. They signed.

———

In fact, they had got a very good deal. The Anglo-Irish Treaty of 1921 effectively conceded full independence to Southern Ireland. Its provisions went way beyond what was on offer in the Home Rule Act of 1914 or the Government of Ireland Act. The Irish Free State, as it was to be known, was to be fiscally and politically independent to a degree undreamed of by the home rulers ten years earlier.

The problem lay not in the substance of the deal, but in its wrapping. In order to appease the Tory backbenchers, Lloyd George had to sell it as having an imperial context: thus the oath of allegiance and the presence of a governor-general representing the king. But the very things that mollified the Tories outraged the republicans in Ireland. The whole focus of opposition to the Treaty lay in the oath of allegiance.

Partition was not a big issue for the anti-Treaty people. They assumed like everyone else that the

Boundary Commission would produce such transfers of land and population from Northern Ireland to the Free State as to fatally destabilise the North.

At any rate, the Treaty split Sinn Féin. In the republican cabinet, it passed only by four votes to three: Griffith, Collins, Barton and W.T. Cosgrave were in favour; de Valera, Cathal Brugha and Austin Stack were opposed. The Dáil debates on the Treaty went on for almost a month, either side of Christmas, until eventually it was approved on 7 January 1922 by the ominously narrow margin of 64 to 57.

Why did nationalists, some of whom could have accommodated themselves to a form of home rule barely ten years earlier, now oppose the Anglo-Irish Treaty with such passion? Everything that had happened since 1912 had raised the stakes. The Great War had radicalised a generation, especially those who chose not to answer Redmond's call to arms in France. The Easter Rising was the central event of that radicalising process. Regardless of its conspiratorial and undemocratic provenance, it now stood as the foundation moment of a new national-ism, explicitly republican in ambition. There were martyrs who might not be betrayed, whose sacrifice might not be dishonoured. And whatever the Treaty had delivered, it was not a republic.

That said, it furnished the substance of republican independence. The ease with which de Valera was later to move the new state from dominion to republican status is evidence of that. Why had the British baulked at conceding the symbolism of a republic? It was an idea

Arthur Griffith. One can understand Yeats' cruel description: 'Griffith staring in hysterical pride'. *National Library of Ireland*

too advanced, not just for the Tory backbenchers—for whom most ideas are too advanced—but also for the other dominions within the existing British Empire. There was no analogue in the contemporary British imagination for such a possibility. Just as the British were now prepared to concede vastly more than in 1912, it would take more time before they could comfortably accommodate the idea of a fully republican state in what had so recently been part of the British metropole.

As to the anti-Treaty republicans, their concentration on the symbolic value of the oath derived from two sources, the Church and the Fenians. Ireland was an intensely Catholic society, in which the cultural variety of Catholicism practised was itself authoritarian, rigorous and legalistic. Even school children were introduced to Catholic apologetics, a series of questions and (more important) answers on religious and moral matters which were orthodox in substance and legalistic in form. In such a culture, the dishonouring of a solemn oath was a serious matter. For many on the anti-Treaty side, that meant that they had to stand by their oath of allegiance to the Republic at all costs. And that was simply not compatible with the Treaty. As for the Fenians, the importance of oath-taking and oath-honouring in what had been a secret society for so long should not be discounted.

With all that, most of the IRB supported the Treaty, influenced no doubt by Michael Collins, the head of the organisation. Likewise, most of the officers in the IRA— those in the best position to know how precarious their military position had been immediately before the Truce—were pro-Treaty. But it was clear that there was a large minority of officers and men who were opposed.

———

A series of efforts aimed at avoiding open conflict between the parties occupied the leaderships from January to June 1922. Under the terms of the Treaty, the Irish Free State was to come into formal existence one year after signature, on 6 December 1922. In the meantime, a Provisional Government was put in place with Michael Collins as Chairman and Minister for Finance. Its membership overlapped with the Dáil government, not recognised formally by the British, headed by Arthur Griffith as President. He had assumed this office following the Treaty vote in the Dáil, which had precipitated de Valera's resignation.

By the end of March, Rory O'Connor, speaking on behalf of the 'Irregulars' (the anti-Treaty IRA), repudiated the authority of the Dáil as having betrayed republican legitimacy. The next day, anti-Treatyites wrecked the printing presses of the *Freeman's Journal*, a nationalist paper that supported the Treaty. By early April, the Irregulars had appointed Liam Lynch as their chief-of-staff. Rory O'Connor led a platoon which seized control of the Four Courts and Kilmainham Jail in Dublin in a gesture so redolent of 1916 that it was unmistakeable.

All was not yet lost, although clearly the situation was deteriorating. Collins and de Valera remained in contact in the hope that politics could find a way of stabilising the situation before the military men took over. It was in vain. De Valera was increasingly sidelined by the Irregular militants. He disappears as a significant figure until after the civil war.

In the meantime, the pro-Treaty IRA were in the process of forming themselves into the National Army under the command of the ubiquitous Collins. In late June 1922, Irregulars based in the Four Courts captured the deputy chief of staff of the National Army, Lt-General J.J. 'Ginger' O'Connell. This was the proximate *casus belli.*

Even then, Collins was reluctant to move. It was the British, horrified that the new constitutional arrangements they had agreed might result in serial chaos and instability, who forced his hand. On 28 June 1922, the National Army of the Irish Free State launched artillery fire at the Four Courts garrison. The civil war was on.

06 | TWO STATES

The Four Courts garrison held out for two days only. On the 30th, they abandoned it, pausing only to set booby-trap explosives in the building, which destroyed the Public Record Office. It was the most outrageous act of cultural vandalism in modern Irish history: Rory O'Connor had been apprised of the importance of the PRO. He could not plead accident or ignorance. Not only was the Four Courts the most imposing monumental building in a city sadly lacking many, the PRO was the greatest single historical archive in the country. It had manuscript deposits dating back to the twelfth century. This irreplaceable treasure store was incinerated. Thus those who would have regarded themselves as the most incorruptible patriots destroyed the key to their country's past and the means of telling its history.

By 5 July, the Provisional Government had full control of the capital, following a fire fight and shoot-out in O'Connell Street that claimed the life of Cathal Brugha. Brave as a lion and reckless, he refused an order to surrender and charged into the street from the building he had been occupying, straight into a storm of machine-gun fire.

Before July was out, Collins' National Army had taken the cities of Waterford and Limerick. Cork followed in early August, taken from the seaward side. By the middle of that month, no significant centre of population lay in Irregular hands. Moreover, their campaign was largely confined to the southern province of Munster. The rest of the country was under the firm control of the Provisional Government. The civil war, therefore, focused on a rural campaign designed to root out guerrilla resistance in what remained of the 'Munster Republic'.

It is worth emphasising the ease with which the Provisional Government and the National Army established their military authority. Formally, the civil war lasted for eleven months, from June 1922 to May 1923. In fact, the outcome was decided in the first six weeks. Even in their Munster heartland, the Irregulars could hardly hope for victory. The Provisional Government's position was grounded democratically: there was no doubt that the people were substantially in favour of accepting the Treaty. An election held in June had returned 58 pro-Treaty TDs, 36 anti-Treaty and 34 others, most of them prepared to support the Provisional

Government. The circumstances in which the election had been held were less than perfect—a pre-election pact between de Valera and Collins to rig the Sinn Féin candidate list in proportion to the numbers in the outgoing Dáil had been repudiated by Collins at the last minute. Still, there could be no doubt where democratic support lay. The Irregulars had no mandate.

The National Army numbered about 15,000 with a further 35,000 available in a Volunteer Reserve. They were supplied with arms by the British: artillery pieces; machine guns; 12,000 rifles plus thousands of revolvers and grenades. The Irregulars probably did not number more than 10,000 men—the Provisional Government's figure of 13,000 was almost certainly an exaggeration—with no more than 7,000 rifles between them.

By the end of 1922, the process of mopping up remaining Irregular redoubts was well advanced. The Provisional Government did not scruple to take the gloves off. It introduced internment without trial. It decreed the death penalty for anyone found in possession of illegal arms. It established military courts. As with all such conflicts, atrocities were committed by both sides. The government executed Irregular prisoners. Erskine Childers, the Englishman turned Irish republican, was shot in November for having in his possession a handgun given to him by Michael Collins before the split. At Ballyseedy, near Tralee, Co. Kerry, nine republican prisoners were taken from the local barracks and tied to a mine which was then detonated under them. Miraculously, one of them survived. In all, the

Provisional Government executed seventy-seven republican prisoners. The severity of its measures and their
unrelenting quality contributed to the speed and com-
pleteness of its victory, but it left a bitterness that lasted
for generations and still subsists in some quarters.

The civil war also claimed the lives of Arthur Griffith
and Michael Collins. Griffith collapsed with a cerebral
haemorrhage on 12 August 1922. He was only fifty-two.
Even more shocking was the death of Michael Collins,
twenty years his junior, ten days later. He was on a tour
of duty of his native West Cork in his capacity as
commander-in-chief of the National Army. It may be
supposed that as he passed among neighbours, the odd
glass was put in his hand. Whether it was Dutch courage
or not, his decision to engage with a group of Irregulars
who had lain in ambush all day was reckless. (Ironically,
they were on the point of abandoning their watch in
despair at his ever appearing.) His convoy could have
accelerated out of the ambush. Instead, he chose to
stand and fight. The action lasted nearly an hour.
Towards the end of that time, a ricochet bullet hit him
in the head and he died that night.

Collins was the fallen hero if ever there was one. He
was mourned on all sides. He had been the most
remarkable person thrown up by the entire turmoil of
the Irish Revolution. He was a brilliant administrator, a
ruthless counter-intelligence chief, a politician and soldier.
He was a force of nature straight out of romantic
fiction. He died two months short of his thirty-second
birthday. It was the boisterous, rambunctious Collins

The destruction of the Four Courts during the Civil War. *RTÉ Stills Library*

who was so often remembered afterwards. But the eloquently reflective words he wrote to a friend on the night he signed the Treaty convey a more profound sensibility, as well as a chilling prophecy:

> *When you have sweated, toiled, had mad dreams, hopeless nightmares, you find yourself in London's streets, cold and dank in the night air. Think—what have I got for Ireland? Something which she has wanted these past seven hundred years. Will anyone be satisfied at the bargain? Will anyone? I tell you this: early this morning I signed my death warrant. I thought at the time how odd, how ridiculous—a bullet may just as well have done the job five years ago.*

The war had more or less petered out by early 1923. It remained only for the death of the commander-in-chief of the Irregulars, Liam Lynch, in April to bring it to an end. There was only one significant action after that, although the government executed its last two prisoners as late as 2 May. The formal order to cease fire and dump arms came on 24 May. In that sense, the civil war did not so much end as subside. It had caused immense material and economic damage and the loss of over 900 lives. It was also the issue around which the party political system in the Free State, later to become the Republic, crystallised. The essential line of political cleavage was to be defined by acceptance of or opposition to the Treaty and consequently by the side taken in the civil war. The two largest parties in modern Ireland,

Fianna Fáil and Fine Gael, are the successors of the anti-Treatyites and the pro-Treatyites respectively. There is an irony in that, of course: the losers in the civil war became in time the dominant party in the state.

———

With the end of the civil war and the restoration of a nervous normality in Northern Ireland, the Irish Revolution may be said to have reached its conclusion. In a headline sense, that is true. But history is a process, not a drama. There is no formal beginning and end. And in the process that was the Irish Revolution, there were a few loose ends to tie up.

The civil war left the Irish Free State with a bloated military establishment, far too large for any peacetime purpose or indeed for the slender pockets of the Irish exchequer. In March 1924, the government of W.T. Cosgrave—who had succeeded to the leadership of the pro-Treatyites on the death of Collins—was faced with its first major crisis. It had announced that the army, including the reserve, was to be reduced in size by 50 per cent. This meant a reduction in the officer corps. A number of disaffected officers issued an ultimatum to the government, calling for a stop to demobilisation and a declaration that the government remained dedicated to the establishment of a united Irish republic. One cabinet minister, close to the mutineers, resigned.

Cosgrave was ill and the crisis was handled by his deputy, the Minister for Home Affairs, Kevin O'Higgins. Apart from Collins, he was the most formidable personality on the pro-Treaty side. He had joined the Volunteers in 1915 and had held a variety of positions in Sinn Féin and the Provisional Government. He had been responsible for establishing the new police force to replace the RIC, the Civic Guard or Garda Síochána (Guardians of the Peace). Remarkably, it was to be an unarmed force, a regulation that survived the furnace of the civil war. O'Higgins had acquired a reputation as the hard man of the new administration and an enthusiast for the execution of prisoners. On the contrary, although he acquiesced in them he had a lawyer's bad conscience about extra-legal measures. One of those executed had been best man at O'Higgins' wedding, a particularly grisly detail that convinced many (even on his own side) that he was heartless in his severity.

Whatever the truth of the matter, he was just the man for the crisis that now faced the government. No democratic government could submit to ultimatums from the military, no matter how justified the grievance. He stated baldly that 'those who take the pay and wear the uniform of the state...must be non-political servants of the state'. He had the ringleaders arrested and he set up a commission of enquiry into the officers' grievances. This delicate balance was disturbed when a group of army officers attempted to arrest armed dissidents in Dublin. They were not acting on orders from O'Higgins or from Mulcahy, the Minister for Defence,

The elite of the new state at Michael Collins's funeral (from left): Richard Mulcahy, Kevin O'Higgins, J.J. 'Ginger' O'Connell, Sean MacEoin. *RTÉ Stills Library*

or from O'Duffy, the commander-in-chief of the National Army. Instead, the order had come from lower down, from the adjutant-general. The government fired the adjutant-general and a number of other officers and accepted the resignation of Mulcahy. O'Higgins was determined not just to defeat the dissidents but also those on his own side who acted *ultra vires*.

The Army Mutiny, as it came to be known, was contained by a mixture of firmness and understanding: legitimate grievances were addressed. The demobilisation continued, but the incident had revealed how strong republican passions could be even on the pro-Treaty side. O'Higgins had shown his mettle in standing firm on the basic point of principle and by drawing the sting of an agitation that could have subverted the democratic institutions of the new state. Three years later, he was assassinated in a Dublin suburb by four freelance IRA gunmen, acting without the sanction of their commanders, in what was presumably a revenge attack for his perceived ruthlessness in the civil war. Churchill memorably described him as 'a figure from antiquity cast in bronze'.

————

As the Army Mutiny was being resolved, the Free State government demanded of the British that a Boundary Commission be established under the terms of Article 12 of the Treaty. This followed inconclusive talks between

Cosgrave and Craig, who now refused to nominate a representative to the Commission. What Craig wanted was the status quo. He regarded a Boundary Commission as everyone else did, as a vehicle for the dismemberment of Northern Ireland. The British government therefore had to introduce special legislation to enable it to appoint a commissioner.

Eoin Mac Neill, by now Minister for Education, was the Free State representative. He was joined by J.R. Fisher, a journalist of well-known unionist views, and the chairman, Richard Feetham, a South African judge. Its terms of reference were that it was 'to determine in accordance with the wishes of the inhabitants, so far as may be compatible with economic and geographic conditions, the boundaries between Northern Ireland and the rest of Ireland'. It sat from late 1924 to the summer of 1925, considered 130 submissions and heard the testimony of almost 600 witnesses.

The Commission agreed to issue no account of its deliberations until it had an agreed position. But an inspired leak to the ultra-Tory *Morning Post*, almost certainly the work of the unionist journalist Fisher, betrayed this. Moreover, what it had to reveal was pretty sensational. There was to be no county transfer: Fermanagh and Tyrone, the two counties with Catholic majorities, would remain in Northern Ireland. All that was proposed was the transfer of part of south Co. Armagh to the Free State while a Protestant part of east Co. Donegal would be tipped into Northern Ireland. These were nugatory changes: the land area of Northern

Ireland would reduce by less than 4 per cent and its population by less than 2 per cent.

Mac Neill resigned, crying treachery and bias. The latter accusation was directed at Feetham. But the chairman, like a cautious lawyer, had attended to the precise wording of Article 12 of the Treaty. The wishes of the inhabitants were one thing, but when qualified by economic and geographic questions, they lost some of their force. Thus the retention of Derry and Newry, two border towns with big Catholic majorities, especially if Derry was to be joined in Northern Ireland by part of its natural economic hinterland in east Donegal. To be fair, Feetham's judgement in these matters was inconsistent. His reluctance to make major breaches in the Treaty and the Government of Ireland Act by transferring whole counties or large parts thereof could not be explained by anything in Article 12 or his own terms of reference. A concern for county integrity is likewise hard to explain with reference to the Treaty, and anyway he was proposing to compromise this principle in Donegal and Armagh.

The thing was a mess, compounded by the political storm that the *Morning Post* scoop had broken. Dublin, Belfast and London came to the same conclusion: suppress the draft report of the Boundary Commission and leave the status quo in place. Sir James Craig could hardly have asked for more.

For Cosgrave's government in Dublin, however, it was gall and wormwood. They had stood on the sanctity of the Treaty, had fought a bitter civil war to uphold it, and now it had let them down. The assumption that the Boundary Commission, that will o' the wisp conjured up as an expedient by Lloyd George, would fillet Northern Ireland was shown for the fantasy it was. The humiliating failure of the whole episode cost the government precious political capital. More seriously, it subverted public confidence in the Treaty as 'the freedom to achieve freedom', in Collins's famous formulation during the Treaty debates. It was the first major test of the Treaty in nationalist eyes and it had failed. Its successes, justifying Collins's description just quoted, lay in the unseen future. In the here and now, the government was conscious of a large republican element in their own following, as the Army Mutiny had demonstrated, not to mention the real republicans once more mobilising around de Valera. For republicans, indeed for all nationalists, it seemed as if de Valera's worst fears had been realised: there was no republic but there was partition.

For the moment, Cosgrave's position was secure. Although the anti-Treatyites had retained the magic name Sinn Féin and constituted themselves as an abstentionist party, they still refused to take their seats in the Dáil. They regarded the Free State and its institutions, including its parliament, as a betrayal of the republic and therefore illegitimate. This eased Cosgrave's position in the short term but weakened it fatally in the long term. His party, Cumann na nGaedheal (Association of the Irish), faced no formal opposition in the Dáil from the largest opposition group. There was only the Labour Party and some maverick independents. It therefore had a clear parliamentary run. It did a mighty impressive job of establishing the institutions of the state but it neglected party organisation. In a country with a long tradition of populism and localism, this was its great error.

De Valera had problems of his own. He understood the futility of the abstentionist position, but he was stuck with it for the moment. However, he chafed under its restrictions and cast about for a way to re-enter the political arena. The opportunities opened up by the Boundary Commission debacle made him all the more frustrated. In March 1926, the Sinn Féin ard fheis (annual conference) debated whether abstention was a party principle or merely a tactic that could be set aside as convenience dictated. De Valera, the party leader, supported the latter position. But he lost the vote narrowly. He seems to have been unsurprised by the result, because he and his supporters immediately walked out en bloc without further ado. Some weeks later, in the La Scala theatre, they founded a new republican party, Fianna Fáil (the Soldiers of Destiny).

It still faced a dilemma. In order to take seats in the Dáil, one was obliged to swear the hated oath of allegiance under the terms of the Treaty. This was impossible for Fianna Fáil. However, there was no doubting their popularity with the electorate. They made an impressive showing at their first general election, in June 1927, when they won 44 seats (only three fewer than Cumann na nGaedheal) and 26 per cent of the vote. Sinn Féin, now in the political wilderness reserved for the principled and the pure of thought, returned only five deputies with less than 4 per cent of the vote. There was little doubt where broad republican sympathy lay. From this moment, Sinn Féin more or less disappears as an effective political force until its re-emergence from the shadows in Northern Ireland in the 1980s.

A month after this election, Kevin O'Higgins was murdered. In response, the government passed an Electoral Amendment Act which required all general election candidates to declare their intention to take the oath if elected. Even before the bill was enacted, de Valera recognised the cul de sac that this would force him into. On 11 August 1927, he bit the bullet. He led his TDs to the Dáil and subscribed to the oath while declaring it to be an 'empty formula'. Mind you, de Valera had made quite a shift in five years: what had been worth a civil war in 1922 was deemed 'an empty formula' in 1927. Still, it had to be done: the Gordian Knot had to be cut. And de Valera had shown, not for the first or last time, that he had what it took to acknowledge terrible necessity.

The following day, Fianna Fáil TDs took their seats in Dáil Éireann for the first time. Eleven years after the Rising, the normal usages of parliamentary life were fully restored in nationalist Ireland. If there is any single moment that marks the symbolic end of the Irish Revolution, this is it. Five years later, Fianna Fáil were in government. Eighty years later they still are. In all those eighty years, they have only been out of office for nineteen.

It remains only to turn finally to Northern Ireland. The Irish Revolution began with the Ulster Crisis, with its corrosive effect on the legitimacy of British rule in Ireland. The revolution in the South, culminating with the entry of Fianna Fáil into the Dáil, was a completed process. It dismantled an old authority and replaced it with a new one, whose legitimacy was unquestioned by all except for the holy fools on the wilder margins of militant republicanism.

In the North, however, nothing was settled and the legitimacy of the state was challenged from the start by the one-third Catholic minority. Understanding this, the triumphant Unionists could have made some attempts, however feeble, to wean nationalists from their disaffection. It would have been the wise and liberal thing to do. But wisdom and liberality were foreign to Ulster. The Unionists simply saw an implacable enemy within. They were certainly right in the sense that no honeyed words or blandishments were going to reconcile Northern Ireland Catholics to the state in the short or medium term. But they did not even try. The religious sectarian hatred that each side had for the other was the toxin that made any generous initiative impossible. Northern Ireland was a Petri dish for the cultivation of a raw, crude and vicious sectarianism that coursed like a poison through the bloodstream of an entire society.

This, more than anything else, meant that it hardly occurred to the Unionists to show generosity in their hour of victory. Any individual gesture along these lines

King George v in Belfast for the opening of the first session of the Northern
Ireland Parliament. *Photograph reproduced with the kind permission of the Trustees
of the National Museums Northern Ireland*

would meet with disapproval and exclusion for the person concerned. Instead, nationalists were to be regarded as de facto non-citizens, people never to be trusted and always to be kept in their place. The fact that, in the short run, this was perfectly understandable after the IRA-led mayhem of 1920-23, does not detract from the reality that it sowed dragon's teeth.

At the heart of Unionist rule was a supremacist impulse. The means of expressing it was the Special Powers Act, a piece of legislation that later drew the envious admiration of Hendrik Verwoerd, the architect of apartheid in South Africa, who only wished that he had such an instrument to hand. The person who did have it to hand in Northern Ireland in the 1920s was the Minister of Home Affairs, Richard Dawson Bates. He was a country solicitor of limited talents and less intelligence. At his command, he had the reconstituted police, now the Royal Ulster Constabulary (RUC) and the B Specials. The latter proved very effective in deterring the IRA but from the first it was involved in sectarian murder and serial harassment of Catholics.

If Catholics were excluded, their exclusion was partly chosen by themselves. Nationalist MPs refused to take their seats in the new Belfast parliament until 1926. They then refused to act as His Majesty's Loyal Opposition until the temporary thaw of the mid-1960s. Even then, their hearts were not in it (they were pressurised into doing it by the Dublin government which was attempting a *démarche* with Belfast) and their scepticism was well justified by the events that followed a few years later. As early as 1921, the Cardinal Archbishop of Armagh and Primate of All Ireland, Joseph Logue, was invited to join a proposed commission to review the education system. He declined the invitation. It was a pity: the Minister of Education was Lord Londonderry, a man of generously liberal impulse. Likewise, nationalists stood aloof from a commission to review local government boundaries. The county councils in Fermanagh and Tyrone refused to recognise the state for a while.

Nationalists were in a mighty sulk in Northern Ireland in the 1920s and it did not always do them much good. The local government boundaries review, dominated as it was by Unionists untrammelled by any Nationalist voice, duly produced a gerrymander in their own interest. Moreover, Craig's government abolished proportional representation in local elections, thus setting aside a measure first intended for the protection of the unionist minority in pre-partition Ireland. Now it would have offered a similar protection to nationalist voters in Northern Ireland, so it had to go. PR ensures the proportional representation of minority interests: it is the electoral system that most nearly matches the percentage of seats to the percentage of votes cast.

The British had not trusted any majority in Ireland not to lord it over a minority, so they abandoned the normal straight vote—which gives a 'bounce' to the largest single party—for Irish local elections. It had been in use only since 1919, so it was relatively untested. Still, Craig was taking no chances. Using the tendentious argument that the straight vote was the normal British way of doing things, he abolished PR. This, combined with a lovingly elaborated series of gerrymanders, ensured a disproportionate representation of Unionists at local level. Derry was the most notorious, but by no means the only, example. Under PR, Derry had returned a Nationalist mayor in 1920. He had admittedly given hostages to fortune with the following inaugural speech:

> *Rest assured that mighty changes are coming in Ireland. Do you Protestants wish to play a part in them? The Unionist position is no longer tenable…. Do you not see that Englishmen are prepared to sacrifice you if they can secure the goodwill of the rest of Ireland? Ireland's right to determine her own destiny will come about whether the Protestants of Ulster like it or not.*

With that sort of rhodomontade ringing in his ear, one can understand Craig's desire not to see the Maiden City in the hands of the enemy. But the gerrymander that kept the Londonderry Corporation safe for Unionism until 1968 was utterly shameless. Northern Ireland was to be run as a formal democracy, but one in which it was essential that the 'right' result be arrived at every time.

In 1929, PR was also abolished for parliamentary elections. A few years later, Craig was to boast that they were a 'Protestant parliament and a Protestant state'. Sir Basil Brooke, later to be Prime Minister for Northern Ireland for twenty years, was to tell his constituents:

A group of the new Ulster Special Constabulary (the B Specials) in 1922. *Hulton Archive/Getty Images*

> *There are a great number of Protestants and Orangemen who employed Roman Catholics. I feel that I can speak freely on this subject as I have not a Roman Catholic about my place... I would point out that the Roman Catholics are endeavouring to get in everywhere and are out with all their force and might to destroy the power and constitution of Ulster. There is a definite plot to overthrow the votes of Unionists in the North. I would appeal to loyalists, therefore, wherever possible, to employ Protestant lads and lassies.*

Craig and Brooke were not backwoodsmen, at least not by Ulster standards: they both rose to the highest provincial office and are still revered figures in the unionist memory. One can imagine what the real backwoodsmen thought and said and how thoroughly they approved of the simple brutalities of the B Specials. (They often *were* the B Specials.)

It is true that the Free State did not set a conspicuous example of liberalism in the 1920s, with its rush to introduce literary censorship and to ban divorce. Equally, it is true that Unionist politicians were able to throw such developments in nationalist faces: it was in this context that Craig made his Protestant people remark, proposing a moral equivalence with the 'Catholic people' to the south. But the Unionists had the levers of power. They used them relentlessly in the most narrow interpretation of their own self-interest.

Perhaps there was no way out for either side. The prejudice and hatred ran both ways. Whichever side was

Aftermath: W.T. Cosgrave, the British Prime Minister Ramsay MacDonald and Sir James Craig in 1924. *Topfoto*

on top was going to keep its minority down. Certainly, nothing in Northern Ireland politics in modern times gives one much room for hope. When one surveys the wasted lives and the apartheid society that Northern Ireland has become, and recalls the long, dismal history of rank sectarian hatred, it seems rather too smug retrospectively to lecture earlier generations for failure to resolve problems that remain intractable to this day.

It is a bleak conclusion. There was nothing to be done for Ulster. Partition, unity, home rule, the empire: none of it made any difference. No matter what sovereignty resided on the ethnic frontier, the mutual hatred of the two tribes is the only constant. In that sense, the Irish Revolution—which accomplished a comprehensive change of regime and *mentalité* in the South—left the North untouched.

SELECT BIBLIOGRAPHY

— Bowman, John, *De Valera and the Ulster Question, 1917–73*, Oxford 1982

— Boyce, D. George, *Nineteenth-Century Ireland: The Search for Stability*, Dublin 1990

— Brooke, Peter, *Ulster Presbyterianism: The Historical Perspective 1610–1970*, Dublin 1987

— Bruce, Steve, *The Red Hand: Protestant Paramilitaries in Ireland*, Oxford 1992

— Bull, Philip, *Land, Politics and Nationalism: A Study of the Irish Land Question*, Dublin 1996

— Callanan, Frank, *The Parnell Split 1890–91*, Cork 1992

— Caulfield, Max, *The Easter Rebellion*, Dublin 1995

— Comerford, R.V., *The Fenians in Context: Irish Politics and Society 1848–1882*, Dublin 1985

— Connolly, S.J., ed., *The Oxford Companion to Irish History*, Oxford 1998

— Coogan, Tim Pat, *The IRA*, London 1980

— Coogan, Tim Pat, *Michael Collins: A Biography*, London 1990

— Coogan, Tim Pat, *de Valera: Long Fellow, Long Shadow*, Dublin 1993

— Curran, Joseph M., *The Birth of the Irish Free State, 1921–23*, Alabama 1980

— Dudley Edwards, Ruth, *Patrick Pearse: The Triumph of Failure*, London 1977

— Elliott, Marianne, *The Catholics of Ulster: A History*, London 2000

— Ferriter, Diarmaid, *The Transformation of Ireland 1900–2000*, London 2004

— Fitzpatrick, David, *Politics and Irish Life 1913–21: Provincial Experiences of War and Revolution*, Dublin 1977

— Foster, R.F., *Modern Ireland 1660–1972*, London 1988

— Garvin, Tom, *The Evolution of Irish Nationalist Politics*, Dublin 1981

— Garvin, Tom, *Nationalist Revolutionaries in Ireland*, Dublin 1987

— Garvin, Tom, *1922: The Birth of Irish Democracy*, Dublin 1996

— Hart, Peter, *The IRA and its Enemies: Violence and Community in County Cork 1916–1923*, Oxford 1998

— Hickey, D.J. & Doherty, J.E., eds, *A New Dictionary of Irish History from 1800*, Dublin 2003
— Hopkinson, Michael, *Green Against Green: The Irish Civil War*, Dublin 1998
— Hopkinson, Michael, *The Irish War of Independence*, Dublin 2002
— Jackson, Alvin, *Ireland 1798–1988*, Oxford 1999
— Keogh, Dermot, *Twentieth-Century Ireland: Revolution and State Building*, Dublin 2005
— Lalor, Brian, ed., *The Encyclopaedia of Ireland*, Dublin 2003
— Lyons, F.S.L., *Charles Stewart Parnell*, London 1977
— Lyons, F.S.L., *Culture and Anarchy in Ireland, 1890–1939*, Oxford 1979
— McGee, Owen, *The Irish Republican Brotherhood from the Land League to Sinn Féin*, Dublin 2005
— Maume, Patrick, *D.P. Moran*, Dublin 1995
— Miller, David W., *Church, Station and Nation in Ireland, 1898–1921*, Dublin 1973
— Miller, David W., *Queen's Rebels: Ulster Loyalism in Historical Perspective*, Dublin 1978
— Mitchell, Arthur, *Revolutionary Government in Ireland: Dáil Éireann, 1919–22*, Dublin 1995
— Moody, T.W. ed., *The Fenian Movement*, Cork 1968
— O'Brien, Conor Cruise, *States of Ireland*, London 1972
— O'Day, Alan, *Irish Home Rule, 1867–1921*, Manchester 1988
— Ó Gráda, Cormac, *Ireland and New Economic History 1780–1939*, Oxford 1994
— O'Halpin, Eunan, *The Decline of the Union: British Government in Ireland, 1892–1920*, Dublin 1987
— Stewart, A.T.Q., *The Ulster Crisis: Resistance to Home Rule, 1912–14*, London 1967
— Stewart, A.T.Q., *The Narrow Ground: Aspects of Ulster, 1609–1969*, London 1977
— Townshend, Charles, *Political Violence in Ireland: Government and Resistance since 1848*, Oxford 1983
— Townshend, Charles, *Easter 1916: The Irish Rebellion*, London 2003
— Wright, Frank, *Northern Ireland: A Comparative Analysis*, Dublin 1988

INDEX

(Note: page numbers in italics refer to illustrations and captions)